In this book Matt Has___ ___ ___ ___ opportunity to gather a ___ ___ ___ ___ seasoned pastors, long gone from this visible world. This book can help the reader to think through not just the importance of personal piety and pastoral skill, but also to see examples of how to pursue such things.

Russell Moore
President, The Ethics & Religious Liberty Commission of the Southern
Baptist Convention

The Puritan authors that are well-known – men like Baxter, Owen, Bunyan and Kiffen – and those not so well-known (but who should be better known) were for the most part pastors. Their written works, from one perspective, can thus all be included under the species of pastoral theology. In this branch of theological knowledge they excelled, for they knew their own hearts and were not afraid to apply the Word of God to every manner of human woe and sin. This compendium of Puritan thought about the pastor's life draws then from a rich vein of Christian wisdom, one that is much needed in this day of shallow thinking – even within the church of the Lord Jesus.

Michael A. G. Haykin
Chair and Professor of Church History,
The Southern Baptist Theological Seminary

PRACTICAL WISDOM THE PASTOR'S LIFE FROM THE PURITANS

MATTHEW D. HASTE
& SHANE W. PARKER

FOREWORD BY SINCLAIR B. FERGUSON

CHRISTIAN
FOCUS

Scripture quotations are from *The Holy Bible, English Standard Version*, copyright © 2001 by Crossway Bibles, a publishing ministry of Good News Publishers. Used by permission. All rights reserved. ESV Text Edition: 2011.

Scripture quotations marked KJV are from the *King James Version*.

paperback ISBN 978-1-5271-0367-2
epub ISBN 978-1-5271-0463-1
mobi ISBN 978-1-5271-0464-8

10 9 8 7 6 5 4 3 2 1

First published in 2019
by
Christian Focus Publications Ltd,
Geanies House, Fearn, Ross-shire,
IV20 1TW, Great Britain.

www.christianfocus.com

Cover by Pete Barnsley (CreativeHoot.com)

Images edited by Lindsey Jacobs (lindsey-jacobs.com)

Printed and bound
by Bell & Bain, Glasgow

Contents

Acknowledgements

In a book about a community of leaders, it is especially appropriate to acknowledge the many individuals who have contributed to this work.

We are grateful to Willie MacKenzie, Rosanna Burton, and the rest of the team at Christian Focus for their careful edits and consistent encouragement throughout this project. We want to thank Sinclair Ferguson for his kind, thoughtful foreword, and Lindsey Jacobs for her great work on the various images within the book. At the risk of forgetting a deserving co-laborer, we would also like to thank the following friends for reading early copies of the manuscript and offering valuable feedback: Brian Albert, Blake Batchelor, Will Cornell, David Gentino, Joe Harrod, Drew Hawthorne, Justin Howard, Caleb Pringle, Andre Rogers, Blaise Shields, Bill Starr, Nathan Stewart, and Randy Williamson.

I (Matt) want to thank my wife, Cheyenne – my best friend and brilliant editor. You are a treasure, who makes every day brighter and every sentence better. To Haddon, Anna, and

Addie: thank you for supporting 'Daddy' in all I try to do and for making me laugh along the way. Finally, I want to express my gratitude to my personal pastor heroes, whom I have had the pleasure of serving alongside at Living Hope Baptist Church in Bowling Green, KY and at Midlands Church in Columbia, SC. Thank you for pastoring me and instilling in me a love for the local church.

I (Shane) want to say thank you to Lydia, my beautiful bride and most trusted friend. Tackling each new chapter of our life together is an exhilarating adventure. I am so grateful that we get to navigate the terrain hand in hand. To Wiley and Evie, who always remind me to take joy in things big and small, you inspire me to reach for more. I love being your daddy. Lastly, I want to express my appreciation for Dr. Richard P. Belcher, Sr., without whom I would not have been heartily introduced to the pastors pictured in the pages to follow. Thank you, Doc.

Together, we would like to dedicate this book to Midlands Church of Columbia, South Carolina. By God's grace, we have each had the opportunity to serve as one of your shepherds in different seasons. You are a faithful people and a regular reminder to us both of the kindness of God. To Him be glory in the church and in Christ Jesus throughout all generations!

Foreword

At first sight – or so it sometimes seems – the kingdom of God makes its greatest advances through a single heroic individual of strong faith, extraordinary ability, and enormous courage. But it would be a mistake to think that the Lord's *modus operandi* is to prefer to use isolated individuals, and it is certainly a misreading of the history of the church. Rarely, if ever, does one man stand alone. Elijah thought he did, but seven thousand others were with him refusing to bow the knee to Baal; Athanasius famously stood *contra mundum* – against the world – but he did not stand *solus* – alone. God rarely uses lone rangers. It is more likely that we simply know all too little about their story. For God seems to love to use 'brotherhoods'.

This was certainly true of the men whose life and work feature in these pages. We usually refer to them as 'The Puritans.' That description has left a chill in many a Christian's bones, with the result that they know all they feel they need to know about them – very little! As recently as perhaps fifty or sixty years ago the only Puritan most Christians would have been able to identify was the 'Bedford Tinker' John Bunyan, and the only Puritan book with which they were familiar was his *Pilgrim's Progress*. Even then, 'familiar' may be an exaggeration.

But, then, scratch further down beneath the surface of the men whose stories appear in this marvellous little book and what will you find? This: a divinely created network whose pastor-members, through personal contact, or influence, or by reading each other's books, were bound together in a remarkable spiritual brotherhood which has had only occasional parallels in the English-speaking world.

Many things may strike you as you read about them and sample this fine selection of their writings. One is that they shared a common burden to see God glorified, His Son magnified, and His Spirit honoured by wholesome and practical biblical preaching, wise pastoral counselling, church and family strengthening, and faithful Christian living. They were all, as C.H. Spurgeon said about Bunyan, men whose blood flowed 'bibline.' They were all outstanding spiritual diagnosticians as well as being intimately familiar with the spiritual pharmaceuticals available in Scripture. The worship of the triune God was of supreme importance to them. And – in marked distinction from the contemporary evangelical sub-culture and the preaching that characterises it – they believed that God's word *itself* transforms lives when it is expounded in the power of the Holy Spirit.

These men preached frequently. They also – at least by our standards – preached long. But this was not because there was no other form of entertainment for Christians. No, for them an hour under the ministry of the word applied by the Spirit to their hearts was the best counselling session any individual could experience. For here, they believed, Christ Himself spoke through His word, the hearts of the hearers were exposed, and spiritual wounds healed. Here too secrets known to none other (and sometimes even hidden from or masked by the hearer himself or herself) were brought to light, sins forgiven, guilt alleviated, light given on the way ahead, and affections cleansed and recalibrated. Puritan preaching was an extended, personal counselling session with Christ Himself.

Would it be unfair to say that what we expect today from preachers is short and superficial by comparison, and usually limited to one sermon per week? Without realizing it, we have become the first generation of Christians since the Reformation in the early sixteenth century to believe that a strong, stable, and neighbour-impactful Christian life can be built on such a slender diet. Alas for us modern Christians if we scoff at the length and the many divisions of the Puritan sermons and pity the hearers who listened to them. For we are the ones most to be pitied because we are too spiritually debilitated to absorb what our forefathers revelled in, so undernourished that, as the author of Hebrews shrewdly notes, that we need milk because we cannot take the solid food of substantial biblical exposition with its glorious exaltation of God and its transforming nourishment for the believer.

Those who have lost weight because they are sick are not able to digest food prepared for the vigorous and healthy. Our lamentation should really be for ourselves if, Laodicea-like, we believe we 'have prospered, and ... need nothing' when in fact we are emaciated skeletal believers. If this is our case, then, while these pages are both fascinating and informative, we will find them also to be full of profound challenges to our thinking and living.

If you are ever in a restaurant where the ambiance suggests that the meal will be good (and very possibly more expensive than you are usually willing to pay!), you will probably be impressed by the attention given to the way the food is served on the plate. The quality of the meat or the fish may not be any better as a result; but the combinations of tastes, the way the food is presented, the quality of the china and the utensils, the white tablecloth – all add to the experience. Someone has given time, thought, and care to the way you are being served.

Something similar is true of these pages. Whether you are long-acquainted with the names that appear in them or are entering the world of seventeenth- and eighteenth-century gospel ministry for the first time, you will be grateful to chefs Matthew Haste and Shane Parker for bringing this excellent menu of spiritual food to your table. And perhaps at times you will feel that the chefs' white coats have become those of doctors (which they both are, in matters of theology and pastoral wisdom). For here they also provide us with a diagnosis of our spiritual needs and prescriptions to restore our health.

So now, Dr. Haste and Dr. Parker are waiting to take you to their clinic and introduce you to a remarkable group of their colleagues from the past. Trust them, for they were master physicians of the soul.

Sinclair B. Ferguson
Chancellor's Professor of Systematic Theology,
Reformed Theological Seminary
Teaching Fellow, Ligonier Ministries

1.
The Puritans as Pastors

Take heed of these Puritans, the very pests (or plagues) of the Church and Commonwealth. (James I, 1566–1625)

The Puritans banned bear-baiting not because it harmed the bear, but because it gave pleasure to the spectators. (British historian Thomas Macaulay, 1800–1859)

Puritanism is the haunting fear that someone, somewhere might be happy. (American journalist H. L. Mencken, 1880–1956)

In his fictional correspondence between two demons, C. S. Lewis quipped that 'one of the really solid triumphs of the last hundred years' for the forces of evil has been the increasingly negative connotations associated with the term 'Puritanism.' As the quotes above demonstrate, Lewis had ample evidence to back up his claim. From the wicked perspective of the elder demon, Screwtape, this triumph had rescued 'thousands of humans from temperance, chastity, and sobriety of life.'[1]

---

1   C. S. Lewis, *The Screwtape Letters* (1961; repr., New York: Touchstone, 1996), 47.

Despite the negative press, a resurgence in appreciation for the Puritans occurred in the latter half of the twentieth century, even as modern society drifted further and further from the world they inhabited. Scholars as diverse as Anglican theologian J. I. Packer and Harvard historian Perry Miller have, in Packer's words, 'been meticulously wiping away the mud' from the Puritan name.[2] Subsequent generations have built on their seminal studies, while pastors such as Martyn Lloyd-Jones and Joel Beeke have helped bring their wisdom into the church.

The present work is not a polemic for Puritanism, but it is written from a perspective of genuine appreciation. More specifically, it is rooted in the conviction that today's pastors could learn much from the Puritans. In the modern world of church and ministry, resources abound. There are books available on nearly every aspect of pastoral ministry and from countless perspectives. At times, the emphasis on practical application and effective strategy results in a shallow approach to ministry. Though far from perfect, the Puritans supply a deep reservoir of biblical wisdom and sound doctrine from which today's pastors can draw. The aim of this book is to make that reservoir more accessible to the average pastor.

To appreciate their wisdom, the Puritans must be situated within their original context. This chapter aims to provide a historical and theological introduction to this movement as well as a foundation for the study that follows. It is our prayer that thousands of pastors would be recaptured by the Puritan vision for pastoral ministry. If a recovery of temperance, chastity, and sobriety of life were to follow – that which

---

2   J. I. Packer, foreword to *Worldly Saints: The Puritans as They Really Were*, by Leland Ryken (Grand Rapids: Zondervan, 1986), ix.

Screwtape feared – we would rejoice, even as the demons would surely shudder.

Historical Context

The Puritan movement was the fruit of the Protestant Reformation spreading to England and, eventually, the American colonies. Though the Church of England formally broke from Rome in 1536, many pastors, unsatisfied with the compromises codified under Queen Elizabeth (1533–1603), called for further reform. The name 'Puritan' originated as a pejorative term for anyone who clamored for the theology, practice, and ministry of the Church of England to be purified of its lingering Catholic influences. The Puritans were inspired by the work of the Reformers in Europe and longed to see their own state church reshaped according to biblical standards. To this end, they attempted to reform the ecclesiastical structures of their day and sought to strengthen the church by setting forth a robust vision for personal godliness.

The time in which they ministered was tumultuous in many ways. The history of the movement is tied up with the rise and fall of the British monarchy and, eventually, the settling of the New World. While the term 'Puritan' can be rightly applied to many pastors in this period, it is important to note that the Puritans were a diverse group who lived in varied times. A brief acquaintance with their historical context will help bring their writings and ministries to life.

Some of the early Puritan pastors referenced in this work, such as William Perkins (1558–1602) and Richard Sibbes (1577–1635), served during a period of increasing political tension but enjoyed enough freedom within the Church of England to continue ministering there. It became much more difficult, however, to be a Puritan within the established church after William Laud (1573–1645) was appointed Archbishop of Canterbury in 1633. For some Puritans, such as John Winthrop (1588–1649), Laud's censorship of the press and enforcement of liturgical conformity inspired a move across the Atlantic.

Various political tensions in England eventually culminated in the mid-century Civil War that led to the execution of King Charles I (1600–1649). The years of the British Commonwealth that followed the war then provided a measure of religious liberty under the leadership of the Puritan-minded Oliver Cromwell (1599–1658). A flurry of publications by men such as John Owen (1616–1683) and Stephen Charnock (1628–1680) provided continuity within the movement even as it splintered along ecclesiological lines. Presbyterian-minded Puritans articulated their theology in the influential *Westminster Confession of Faith* (1644), a document later edited and affirmed by both the English Congregationalists (*The Savoy Declaration*, 1658) and the Calvinistic Baptists (*Second London Confession of Faith*, 1689).

After Cromwell's death and the restoration of the monarchy, the new Parliament passed a series of laws in the 1660s that barred such groups from holding public meetings and required their pastors to conform to the standards of the Church of England. As a result, over two thousand ministers with Puritan sentiments were cast from their pulpits and many landed in prison, including John Bunyan (1628–1688) and Richard Baxter (1615–1691).

Eventually, the Glorious Revolution of 1688–1689 established Parliament as the ruling power in England. The subsequent *Act of Toleration* provided legal protection for the Puritans, yet the newfound freedom seemed to open the door to spiritual lethargy and doctrinal decline. Meanwhile, the once-promising New England expedition shifted its attention to the difficulties of frontier life. The Puritan vision continued to live on in the colonies in some sense, particularly in the preaching ministry of men such as Jonathan Edwards (1703–1758), but its influence waned considerably in the years that followed.

Theological Emphases

While the Puritans lived in diverse contexts, several theological convictions were central to the movement. The typical Puritan looked to the Scriptures as the principle authority for faith and practice, sought communion with God daily, and organized his/her theology around the doctrines of grace. These emphases distinguished the Puritans from their contemporaries and provide a general framework for understanding who they were. Quality studies on Puritan theology are available, so the following overview will merely introduce the key issues and provide a foundation for subsequent chapters.[3]

The Puritans sought to build their theology, ecclesiology, and spirituality on the Scriptures alone. Broadly-speaking, this conviction distinguished them at the time from the Quakers, who placed a greater emphasis on the work of the Spirit, and the Church of England, which held a higher view of tradition. This emphasis on viewing the Bible as a sufficient guide for faith and life anchored their understanding of preaching, which was central to the life of the church just as discipleship was central to the home. What the seventeenth-century Baptist William Kiffin (1616–1701) said of his Puritan contemporary John Norcott (d. 1676) could be said of any of the pastors

---

3   For recommended resources, see the list provided at the end of this chapter.

featured in this volume: 'He steered his whole course by the compass of the Word.'[4]

Possessing a robust vision of the Trinity, the Puritans carefully articulated how the Spirit of God made a way for the individual believer to fellowship with the Father and the Son. In his excellent overview of the Puritans, *A Quest for Godliness: The Puritan Vision for the Christian Life*, Packer notes that Owen, for example, focused on the mutual interchange between the Triune God and man, that he was eager to maintain that such communion was only possible through God's initiative, and that the Lord's Table provided a unique opportunity for such fellowship.[5] Owen's emphases are representative of many of his Puritan contemporaries.

Although some theological variation existed within the movement, the majority of Puritans operated within a Calvinistic understanding of the doctrines of grace. Like the Reformers before them, they emphasized man's inability to save himself and called upon sinners to look to the mercy of God. Their sober view of man led to an accompanying emphasis on the work of the Spirit, who promises inner renewal and enables obedience after conversion. On the whole, the Puritans placed their hope in the gracious initiative of God and sought to order all of life, including the work of the pastor, toward His glory.

Bridging the Gap

The aim of this book is to mine the riches of the Puritan legacy in hopes of encouraging and strengthening pastors today. Like

---

4 William Kiffin and Richard Claridge, 'The Epistle Dedicatory,' in John Norcott, *Baptism Discovered Plainly & Faithfully, According to the Word of God*, 3rd ed. (London, 1694), ii.

5 J. I. Packer, *A Quest for Godliness: The Puritan Vision for the Christian Life* (Wheaton, IL: Crossway, 1990), 204-15.

any collection of historical examples, the Puritans are helpful in some areas and less so in others; but the seriousness with which they approached pastoral ministry and the convictions that undergirded their efforts are commendable.

In hopes of making the vast Puritan corpus more accessible, each chapter addresses a particular task of pastoral ministry and highlights how one (or two) Puritan(s) approached that facet of being a pastor. For each category, we asked ourselves, 'Which Puritan might provide a helpful example for how to approach this aspect of ministry?' Our choices were based on maximizing practical wisdom rather than offering a full representation of the Puritan tradition. While other Puritans may have deserved more attention, we have attempted to focus on individual pastors in hopes of introducing them on a personal level. To this end, each chapter begins with basic biographical information to acquaint the reader with the person; the dates and locations provided properly situate each pastor in his historical context.

The Puritans were imperfect shepherds, but they took seriously the business of caring for souls. They served in a different world and at a different time, but their ministries were rooted in Scripture and calibrated toward the glory of God. Rather than dismissing their examples based on inaccurate stereotypes, today's pastors would do well to listen carefully to their stories and consider their ways. As the following quotes demonstrate, many have been inspired by the legacy of the Puritans. Our prayer is that this study will introduce a new generation of pastors to their timeless wisdom.

Ministers never write or preach so well as when under the cross;
the Spirit of Christ and of glory then rests upon them. It was this,

no doubt, that made the Puritans ... such burning and shining lights. (George Whitefield, 1714–1770)

The Puritans, as a body, have done more to elevate the national character than any class of Englishmen that ever lived. (J. C. Ryle, 1816–1900)

By all means, read the Puritans, they are worth more than all the modern stuff put together. (Charles Haddon Spurgeon, 1834–1892)

In a time of failing vision and decaying values, [the Puritans are] a beacon of hope calling us to a radical commitment and action when both are desperately needed. (J. I. Packer, 1926–)

My own experience is that no one comes close to the skill [the Puritans] have in taking the razor-like scalpel of Scripture, and lancing the boils of my corruption, cutting out the cancers of my God-belittling habits of mind, and amputating the limbs of my disobedience. They are simply in a class by themselves. (John Piper, 1946–)

Few, if any, epochs in the history of the Christian church can boast so many outstanding examples of pastoral ministry as the Puritan period of the late sixteenth and seventeenth centuries. (Sinclair Ferguson, 1948–)

Recommended Resources:

Leland Ryken, *Worldly Saints* (1990).

Kelly Kapic and Randall Gleason, *The Devoted Life: An Invitation to the Puritan Classics* (2004).

Joel Beeke and Randall J. Pederson, *Meet the Puritans* (2007).

J. I. Packer, *A Quest for Godliness* (2010).

Joel Beeke and Mark Jones, *A Puritan Theology: Doctrine for Life* (2012).

Michael A. G. Haykin, *The Puritans and Reformers as Spiritual Mentors* (2013).

John Bunyan (1628–1688)

Pastor, Bedford Church (England)

Primary Works

Pilgrim's Progress
Grace Abounding to the Chief of Sinners

Mentor

John Gifford

'Eyes lifted up to heaven, the best of books in his hand, the law of truth written upon his lips, the world behind his back; he stood as if he pleaded with men, and a crown of gold did hang over his head.' (John Bunyan)

2.

The Pastor's Call
with John Bunyan

At the southwest corner of St. Peter's green in the English town of Bedford, a bronze statue sits close to the street. The sculpture was dedicated in 1874, but the man it depicts has cast his shadow over the town since the seventeenth century. The statue embodies not only the town's most-famous resident, but also his vision. The man's eyes are lifted to the heavens, the best of books is in his hands; he bears a grave expression, yet he looks ready to speak a word of truth at any moment, to plead with passersby. This, it seems, is exactly how John Bunyan would want to be remembered.

In fact, his depiction of the ideal pastor supplied the inspiration for the statue. In Bunyan's famous allegory *Pilgrim's Progress*, the first image Christian came upon in the House of the Interpreter was a painting of a man resembling the description above. The host explained that this man was tasked by his Master to stand between men and the world to 'know and unfold dark things'. With his back to the world and his eyes on the heavens, the man was among the select few authorized to guide others along their way to the Celestial City.

This is how Bunyan thought of the work of the pastor. A pastor is a herald proclaiming good news. With Bible in hand, he is entrusted by God to speak truth to the world. He recognizes the seriousness of his task and knows that he labors for a heavenly reward. Several additional characters in Bunyan's allegory complete the picture. Like Evangelist, a pastor leads sinners toward the cross and, if necessary, redirects them when they go astray. Like Help, a pastor lends a hand to others, even if it draws him into the muck and mire of their bad decisions. Like Watchful the Porter, a pastor guides individuals into the church, while faithfully guarding its doors. Like the Shepherds on the Delectable Mountains, a pastor has the privilege of encouraging pilgrims as they journey from this world toward that which is to come.

Bunyan was typical of the Puritans in his veneration of the pastorate. Thomas Goodwin, for example, considered ministry 'the best calling in the world'.[1] William Perkins admitted it was a 'painful calling', but argued, 'no man in no calling hath so special attendance and assistance of God's angels as godly ministers have.'[2] So, how did the Puritans discern who among them was called by God for this great work?

The Puritan Concept of Calling

The Puritans thought about the call to ministry in the context of a Reformation view of vocation. The Reformers had challenged the medieval dichotomy between the sacred and

---

1   *Works of Thomas Goodwin* (1863; repr., Edinburgh: Banner of Truth, 1979), 6:415.

2   William Perkins, *A Treatise of the Dignities and Duties of the Ministry* (London: I. R., 1605), 76.

the secular by encouraging Christians to worship God through their unique vocations. The Puritans further developed this conviction, calling vocation an act of stewardship 'ordained and imposed on man by God for the common good.'[3] In the Puritan mind, God appointed each person to a particular vocation for His own sovereign purposes. If God called a man into the pastorate, the Puritans believed his life would display certain characteristics that confirmed this calling.

Richard Baxter's overview of the essential qualifications of a minister articulated these parameters succinctly. He observed that a minister should possess '(1) understanding and belief of all the essential articles of faith without heresies; (2) tolerable ability to teach these to the people; and (3) sincere godliness to do all this in love and obedience to God.'[4] To this Baxter added a fourth qualification under the label 'lawful calling', by which he meant the invitation of a particular church. The Puritan framework for understanding the call to ministry can be summarized by the following four terms: conviction, competence, character, and confirmation.

Conviction

As part of the Anglican ordination process at the time, prospective pastors were asked if they felt inwardly moved by God to assume the role. Matthew Henry described this *conviction* as a man's 'earnest desire ... for the prospect he has

---

3   William Perkins, *A Treatise of the Vocations or Callings of Men* (Cambridge: John Legat, 1603), 2. Perkins was a leading thinker on this subject and one of the most influential men of his generation. For more on Perkins, see chapter 8.

4   Richard Baxter, *Christian Directory*, in *Practical Works of Richard Baxter* (1846; repr., Morgan, PA: Soli Deo Gloria, 2000), 632. Baxter's approach to pastoral ministry is discussed in chapter 10.

of bringing greater glory to God, and of doing the greatest good to the souls of men by this means,'[5] Considering their contemporaries lazy and corrupt, the Puritans called for a renewal of this passion. As Baxter noted, ministers should be exemplars of doctrine and piety, a concern that slowed Bunyan himself in the process of determining whether or not he could serve in this all-important role.

Competence

The Puritans also believed that pastors must possess the *competence* to preach from the Scriptures, making their meaning plain to the congregation. This required both knowledge of the Bible and dexterity with people. John Owen spoke of the Spirit's work in making a man competent to serve the church. 'Where there are none of those spiritual abilities which are necessary unto the edification of the church,' he argued, 'no outward call or order can constitute any man an evangelical pastor.'[6]

Character

The third distinctive of the Puritan understanding of the call to ministry was the importance of *character*. Owen emphasized such piety in at least three of his five essential qualifications of a minister: 'compassion and love to the flock ... zeal for the glory of God ... [and] some degree of eminent holiness.'[7] All that qualifies a minister, he noted, is patterned after Christ

---

5   Matthew Henry, *Commentary on the Whole Bible,* vol. 6 (New York: Fleming H. Revell, 1950), 814-15.

6   John Owen, *The True Nature of a Gospel Church*, in *Works of John Owen,* ed. William H. Goold (1850–1853; repr., Edinburgh: Banner of Truth, 1968), 16:49.

7   Owen, *True Nature of a Gospel Church*, 49.

Himself. In Bunyan's portrait of the ideal pastor, the man had his back turned to the world that he might better fix his eyes on God. Such is the posture of a godly minister.

Confirmation

Finally, the Puritans placed a great deal of emphasis on the external *confirmation* of the church. In calling a pastor, a church confirmed that the man possessed the competence, character, and conviction necessary to serve. Such qualities were evidence of the work of God in his life and the church exercised its authority in publicly calling him into the role. As Perkins summarized, 'If any ask, how he shall know when God calls him, I answer, God calls ordinarily by his church, her voice is his.'[8]

The Puritans did not elevate one aspect of calling above the rest but rather sought a confluence of characteristics that demonstrated God's wise hand of preparation. When a man established the necessary qualifications – conviction to lead and teach, competence for the work, Christ-like character, and the confirmation of God's people – then, and only then, could he consider himself called to the ministry.

Bunyan's Call to Ministry

John Bunyan's journey into the pastorate is a helpful illustration of how these principles worked out in one man's life. Bunyan was the son of a village tinker destined for a life in the family business until God intervened. Possessing little formal education, he was an indulgent and rebellious youth. However, after reading two classic Puritan works that left him convicted of his sin, he began to attend church and observe

---

8   Perkins, *Treatise of Dignities and Duties of Ministry*, 105.

the Sabbath with feverish devotion.[9] Soon after, he overheard a group of women – who belonged to the local Baptist church in Bedford – discussing the new birth. Their description of a personal relationship with Jesus alarmed him. He was aware that he knew no such comfort, and he did not know where to find it.

For the next several years, Bunyan wrestled with his faith, until finally, in the early 1650s, he experienced true conversion. The Bedford congregation and its pastor, John Gifford, were instrumental in his spiritual awakening, as was his growing appetite for the Scriptures. Several years later, some observant members of his church began to recognize his spiritual potential. As he recorded in his spiritual autobiography *Grace Abounding to the Chief of Sinners*, they 'did perceive that God had counted me worthy to understand something of his will in his holy and blessed word, and had given me utterance in some measure, to express what I saw to others, for edification.' So, they asked Bunyan to provide a 'word of exhortation' at an upcoming meeting, which in turn was well-received. As Bunyan later reported, 'I discovered my gift amongst them' as the congregation was 'both affected and comforted.' After he was asked to preach several more times, he began to pray and fast for wisdom. When the church appointed him to a more regular preaching role, he confessed, 'I did evidently find in my mind a secret pricking forward thereto.' His heart set upon 1 Corinthians 16:15 in particular, which, in the Authorized Version that Bunyan read, spoke of the apostles having 'addicted themselves to the ministry of the saints.' Bunyan, feeling this same desire growing in his own heart and continuing to see fruit from his labors, concluded, 'These things, therefore, were

---

9   For more on these books, see the opening page of chapter 5.

another argument unto me, that God [had] called me to, and stood by me in this work.'[10]

Bunyan was first recognized for his character and then tested to evaluate his competence. As the church confirmed his gifts, he began to develop the conviction that he longed to serve the Lord in this way. The sum of those elements led Bunyan to conclude that he was, indeed, called to ministry.[11] Bunyan remained confident in this call even while confined to the Bedford jail that his statue faces today. He would become one of the most highly-regarded preachers and influential authors of the Puritan era, but only after he was sure he possessed the necessary qualifications.

Called and Qualified

The Puritan perspective on calling is not above critique but the following brief commendations highlight the wisdom their writings offer for pastors today. Each point provides a helpful contrast to the approach of many modern evangelicals.

First, *the Puritans considered the call to ministry in the context of a full-orbed doctrine of vocation*. Many in the church today approach this question through the lens of the sacred-secular divide of medieval thought. Assuming the inherent superiority of ministry over other vocations, they seem to ask themselves, 'Do I have a special call from God into ministry or am I left to figure out a career on my own?' The Puritans, on the other hand, recognized that all people are called by God and gifted for particular vocations.

---

10   John Bunyan, *Grace Abounding to the Chief of Sinners*, in *Works of John Bunyan* (Edinburgh: Banner of Truth Trust, 1991), 1:36.

11   The story of Bunyan's contemporary, the London pastor Frances Bampfield (d. 1683) provides a helpful parallel. See Frances Bampfield, *A Name, an After-One* (London: John Lawrence, 1681).

Second, *the Puritan process for discerning one's calling was far more objective than subjective.* They encouraged individuals to consider how God had gifted them, what opportunities lay before them, and especially, how others responded to them. This process, guided by the church, was instrumental in Bunyan's development. This leads to a related point.

The Puritans emphasized external rather than internal confirmation. They did not ask, 'How do you feel about this?' but rather 'How have you seen others respond?' This entrusted primary responsibility to the collective wisdom of the church and its leaders. Such a process forces a man to look outside himself and protects him in some way from self-deception.

Finally, *the Puritan approach was multi-faceted rather than mystical or minimalistic.* Rather than over-simplifying the process or elevating one aspect of calling above the rest, the Puritans encouraged young men to approach the question from several angles. The four characteristics – conviction, competence, character, and confirmation – held relatively equal weight in helping someone determine if God had qualified him for vocational ministry. This inclination may be the most useful piece of wisdom one can gain from the Puritans today. Their approach highlighted the various ways in which God typically prepares a man for ministry.

The 'Four Cs' emphasized in this chapter parallel a set of c-words more commonly known today. In the twentieth century, gemologists identified 'Four Cs' that help classify the quality of a diamond – cut, carat, color, and clarity. Each characteristic serves as an indicator of the overall quality of the stone, but no single measurement is sufficient on its own to determine the diamond's value. A wise jeweler examines a diamond from all angles, fixing trained eyes on potential imperfections or subtle deficiencies to determine its fitness for serving as a ring's centerpiece. A high mark in one category could skew the evaluation for a novice, but an expert knows to grade the stone across all four categories.

The parallel to the four themes of this chapter is instructive. Just as jewelers learn to evaluate diamonds through a set of established categories, so we must train young men to evaluate themselves. Rejecting a simplistic lens, they must look at their lives from all angles – and get help from others – to discover if God has truly qualified them for the work of ministry. Bunyan and the Puritans understood the high calling of the pastorate and were eager to protect the office. They offer a wise example for helping young men determine if they are called by God to serve as pastors today.

Thomas Goodwin (1600–1680)

Pastor, Holy Trinity Church; President, Magdalen College, Oxford

Primary Work

The Heart of Christ in Heaven towards Sinners on Earth

Mentors

Richard Sibbes (1577–1635) and John Preston (1587–1628)

'In Christ are treasures that will require digging to the end of the world.' (Thomas Goodwin)

Stephen Charnock (1628–1680)

Proctor, New College, Oxford; Chaplain to Henry Cromwell;
Pastor, Nonconformist Congregation at Crosby Hall, London

Primary Works

The Existence and Attributes of God
Christ Crucified: The Once-for-All Sacrifice

Mentor

Thomas Goodwin (1600–1680)

3.

The Pastor's Bible
with Thomas Goodwin
and Stephen Charnock

Among modern guides to the Puritans, few can match the insight of J. I. Packer. In *A Quest for Godliness*, Packer surveys the lives and thoughts of Puritan pastors and writers, highlighting how their veneration of the Bible shaped their ministries:

> To the Puritan the Bible was in truth the most precious possession that this world affords. His deepest conviction was that reverence for God means reverence for Scripture, and serving God means obeying Scripture. To his mind, therefore, no greater insult could be offered to the Creator than to neglect his written word; and, conversely, there could be no truer act of homage to him than to prize it and pore over it, and then to live out and give out its teaching.[1]

Living out and giving out the Bible's teaching is an appropriate summary for the driving pursuit of both Thomas Goodwin

---

1   J. I. Packer, *A Quest for Godliness: The Puritan Vision for the Christian Life* (Wheaton, IL: Crossway, 1990), 98.

and Stephen Charnock. Their lives ran parallel to one another – their paths intersected early and they died within the same year (1679–1680) – as they each called for the study of this most precious of possessions, the Bible.

Studying Biblical Texts with Thomas Goodwin

Goodwin was born in Norfolk and later educated at Christ's College, Cambridge. It was here that he came under the preaching and influence of Richard Sibbes (1577–1635) and John Preston (1587–1628) at Holy Trinity Church, Cambridge. Both Sibbes and Preston left indelible marks on Goodwin's approach to theology and preaching, as 'Christ-centered preachers who advocated a distinctly Reformed position on theology, the Scriptures, and the church's creeds and confessions.'[2]

Converted in 1620, Goodwin maintained a commitment to these distinctive contours of theology and practice inherited from Sibbes and Preston. In 1628, he succeeded his mentors as lecturer at Trinity Church, a post he held for six years before stepping down under pressure to conform to the liturgical requirements of William Laud. After brief stints in London and the Netherlands, he returned to London in 1641.

While serving in a pastoral capacity in the city, Goodwin was appointed to the Westminster Assembly in 1643. Although he maintained conviction of independent church government, he garnered the admiration of the Presbyterian brothers who formed the majority of the participants.[3] Goodwin was

---

2   Joel Beeke and Mark Jones, eds., *A Habitual Sight of Him: The Christ-Centered Piety of Thomas Goodwin* (Grand Rapids: Reformation Heritage, 2009), 7.

3   Joel Beeke and Randall J. Pederson, *Meet the Puritans* (Grand Rapids: Reformation Heritage, 2007), 270.

additionally appointed President of Magdalen College in 1650, while John Owen was placed as Dean of Christ Church, Oxford. The two men shared chaplain responsibilities for Oliver Cromwell, the head of state in England, as well as a pulpit on Sundays.

Remembering Goodwin's final days before his death in 1680, Thomas Goodwin, Jr., later recounted that his father declared, 'Christ cannot love me better than he doth; I think I cannot love Christ better than I do; I am swallowed up in God.'[4]

In his book *Thirteen Appreciations*, Scottish pastor Alexander Whyte (1836–1921) sought to acknowledge those theologians and pastors who had most impacted his own ministry. He notes that he was in his third year as a student at New College in Edinburgh when he encountered Goodwin's writings. Speaking to a group of college students years later, Whyte fondly remarked, 'I will here say with simple truth that his Works have never been out of my hands down to this day.' That initial encounter with Goodwin's striking approach to the study and interpretation of the Bible is vividly captured in Whyte's depiction: 'But there is a grappling power; there is a studying down of the passage in hand and, withal, there is a height, and a depth, and fertilizing suggestiveness in Goodwin.'[5]

This persistent 'studying down' of the passage is perhaps nowhere better seen than in Goodwin's documented preaching from Paul's letter to the Ephesians. The lasting impression made by these sermons on Whyte was so deep that he declared,

4   'Memoir of Thomas Goodwin, D. D., by his Son,' in *Works of Thomas Goodwin* (Grand Rapids: Reformation Heritage, 2006), 2:xxiv-xxxv.

5   Alexander Whyte, *Thirteen Appreciations* (London: Oliphant, Anderson and Ferrier, 1913), 161.

'For not even Luther on the Galatians is such an expositor of Paul's mind and heart as is Goodwin on the Ephesians.'[6] This imploring sense in Goodwin is seen from the outset of his work in Ephesians, as he comments on Paul's salutation (Eph. 1:1-2) when exhorting his congregation to see this epistle as God's word for them:

> Know, therefore, that when you read any epistle, the whole weight of their apostolical spirit and authority in them is to fall upon all our consciences and spirits, as it did on theirs, unto these purposes, both to assure our hearts of the unerring truth of every tittle of them, and their word in their writings to be as true as God is ... as also to receive all their injunctions and commands therein, as coming with the same apostolical authority that it did to those to whom they were by name written, and as immediately warranting us in all those practices which their living commands did put them upon.[7]

Goodwin also founded and pastored an Independent church in London. Charnock, who was a member of that congregation, modeled his own interpretive and teaching labors after his pastor. While Goodwin is highly regarded for his exegetical precision, along with a masterful ability to preach with passion, Charnock is best known for his ability to systematically address biblical doctrines.

Studying Biblical Doctrines with Stephen Charnock

As a pastor, those you lead will sometimes ask which books have had the greatest impact on your life and ministry. For me,

---

6   Whyte, ibid., 162.

7   Thomas Goodwin, 'An Exposition of the First Chapter of the Epistle to the Ephesians,' in *Works of Thomas Goodwin* (Grand Rapids: Reformation Heritage, 2006), 1:6.

one such book was A. W. Pink's *The Attributes of God*. I knew very little about biblical doctrine when I picked up that slim paperback as a college student, and I was stunned by Pink's observations about the unfettered grandeur and unparalleled beauty of God. However, there was another element to that work which made it so impactful. The author offered block quotes from some beginning-to-be-familiar names (e.g., Jonathan Edwards, C. H. Spurgeon), but the chapter on God's holiness had a series of quotes from a less-familiar voice – Stephen Charnock. These were the first words that I read from the Puritan's pen:

> Not all the vials of judgment that have or shall be poured out upon the wicked world, nor the flaming furnace of a sinner's conscience, nor the irreversible sentence pronounced against the rebellious demons, nor the groans of the damned creatures, give such a demonstration of God's hatred of sin, as the wrath of God let loose upon His Son. Never did Divine holiness appear more beautiful and lovely than at the time our Savior's countenance was most marred in the midst of His dying groans. This He Himself acknowledges in Psalm 22. When God had turned His smiling face from Him, and thrust His sharp knife into His heart, which forced that terrible cry from Him, 'My God, My God, why hast Thou forsaken me?' He adores this perfection – 'Thou art holy.'[8]

This caliber of intense insight and piercing application was virtually unknown to me. Charnock's work in *Discourses upon the Existence and Attributes of God*, from which this excerpt

---

8   Stephen Charnock, *The Existence and Attributes of God*, quoted in A. W. Pink, *The Attributes of God* (Grand Rapids: Baker, 1975), 43.

was drawn, set an attractive standard for what it meant for me to treat the text of the Bible with hot-hearted, active reverence.

Born in London in 1628, Charnock was inclined toward study from an early age. He entered Cambridge in 1642, at the age of fourteen. After eventually serving as senior proctor at Oxford from 1652–1656, he left for Ireland, where he fulfilled the role of chaplain to the governor, Henry Cromwell (1628–1674). He served several churches in Ireland, before returning to England in 1660. For the next fifteen years, he spent his vocational energies practicing medicine, until he became co-pastor of a congregation in London, alongside Thomas Watson (c.1620–1686). He remained in this pastoral role until his death in 1680.

Perhaps the most notable thread through each season of Charnock's life was his dedication to and reputation for study. Not only did he dedicate approximately a dozen hours, five days a week, to research, he also 'wrote out everything he proposed to say in public.'[9] Since this is the case, Charnock's sermonic discourses were thoroughly detailed. Packer notes that 'each built on a text and laid out with doctrine, reason (exposition and defense), and use (application) in the standard Puritan manner.'[10] It was Charnock's position that studying the doctrines of the Bible carefully could yield soul-nourishing sustenance for a life dedicated to the glory of God.

Studying the Bible with the Puritans
Men like Goodwin and Charnock accepted that the Bible was *the written word from* God, and they assumed that it taught *what to believe about* God as well as *how to practice what was*

---

9   J. I. Packer, *Puritan Portraits* (Fearn, Scotland: Christian Focus), 49.
10   Packer, *ibid.*, 49.

believed. A distinctive among the Puritans was a keen awareness of the need to be both unswervingly biblical and resolutely experiential ('experimental' was the term most commonly used in their day). The primacy of the Bible in study and life was 'Puritanism's hallmark'.[11]

Packer goes on to summarize the 'rules' for interpretation that followed from these presuppositions: (1) interpret Scripture *literally and grammatically*; (2) interpret Scripture *consistently and harmonistically*; (3) interpret Scripture *doctrinally and theocentrically*; (4) interpret Scripture *christologically and evangelically*; (5) interpret Scripture *experimentally and practically*; and (6) interpret Scripture *with a faithful and realistic application*.[12] In order to emulate their approach, Packer suggests asking certain questions of every text that is studied. In Table 3.1 below, I have adapted these questions and connected them with the 'rule' emphases outlined above.

Table 3.1

Interpretive Rule	Interpretive Question(s)
Interpret Scripture literally and grammatically.	What do these words actually mean?
Interpret Scripture consistently and harmonistically.	What light do other Scriptures throw on this text? Where and how does it fit into the total biblical revelation?
Interpret Scripture doctrinally and theocentrically.	What truths does it teach about God, and about man in relation to God?

---

11   Packer, *ibid.*, 49.

12   Packer, *ibid.*, 101-05.

Interpret Scripture christologically and evangelically.	How are these truths related to the saving work of Christ, and what light does the gospel of Christ throw upon them?
Interpret Scripture experimentally and practically.	What experiences do these truths delineate, or explain, or seek to create or cure? For what practical purpose do they stand in Scripture?
Interpret Scripture with a faithful and realistic application.	How do they apply to myself and others in our own actual situation? To what present human condition do they speak, and what are they telling us to believe and do?

In each case, the questions asked of the text introduce clarity in understanding and application. This clarity of thought and practice should nourish the reader's own soul, while also establishing a firm footing from which to teach and preach the Bible.

Studying the Bible to Teach the Bible

In *On Christian Teaching*, Augustine of Hippo (354–430) argued for the study of the Bible to include intentional action toward instruction. He writes, 'There are two things on which all interpretation of scripture depends: the process of discovering what we need to learn, and the process of presenting what we have learnt.'[13] Pastors study the Bible in order to teach it to

---

13   Augustine, *On Christian Teaching* (New York: Oxford, 1997), 8.

others. Centuries later, Whyte reflected on Goodwin's similarly tight connection between robust study and faithful teaching:

> Full as Goodwin always is of the ripest scriptural and Reformation scholarship; full as he is of the best theological and philosophical learning of his own day and of all foregoing days; full, also, as he always is of the deeper spiritual experience – all the same, he is always so simple, so clear, so direct, so un-technical, so personal, and so pastoral.[14]

As we study the biblical text and explore sound doctrine, may an outcome of these demanding efforts be that our teaching is clear, personal, and pastoral. Pastors must endeavor to both discover and present the truth for the sake of the church.

---

14   Whyte, *ibid.*, 171.

John Owen (1616–1683)

Private and Military Chaplain, Vice Chancellor of Oxford
University; Dean of Christ Church, Oxford

Primary Works

The Death of Death in the Death of Christ
Mortification of Sin
Communion with God
Discourse on the Holy Spirit, Of Temptation
The Glory of Christ

Mentor

Thomas Barlow (1608–1691)

'In the divine Scriptures, there are shallows and there are deeps;
shallows where the lamb may wade, and deeps where the
elephant may swim.' (John Owen)

4.

The Pastor's Doctrine
with John Owen

Perhaps best known for his legendary poem *Paradise Lost*, famed English poet John Milton (1608–1674) understood the goal of teaching in this way:

> The end then of learning is to repair the ruins of our first parents by regaining to know God aright, and out of that knowledge to love him, to imitate him, to be like him, as we may the nearest by possessing our souls of true virtue, which being united to the heavenly grace of faith makes up the highest perfection.[1]

Knowing God 'aright' is the foundation for living for His glory and knowing God comes through the study of sound doctrine.

If we are to teach well, our pastoral lives and instruction must be in harmony with sound doctrine (Titus 2:1). This aim must include both orthodoxy (faithful belief) and orthopraxy (faithful practice). John Owen was a monumental Puritan figure who offers a pastoral model toward this end.

---

1   John Milton, 'Of Education,' in *Complete Prose Works of John Milton* (New Haven, CT: Yale University Press), 2:366.

The Varied Ministry of John Owen

Owen was born the second son of Henry Owen, in Stadham, just a few miles southeast of Oxford. Henry was a Puritan minister. John was likely influenced by his father's life and vocation, but he was reserved in what he recounted of his early life. At the age of twelve he enrolled at Queen's College, Oxford. There he earned a Bachelor of Arts in 1632 and a Master of Arts in 1635.

Owen's academic preparation led him first to serve as a private chaplain, which in God's providence shaped him both as a gospel minister and a budding writer. Joel Beeke and Randall J. Pederson note, 'At the age of twenty-six, Owen began a forty-one-year writing span that produced more than eighty works.'[2] Centuries later, his writing continues to instruct and influence Christians in hearty doctrinal understanding and application.

His career would also involve military chaplain service on Oliver Cromwell's expedition to Ireland in 1649. He was then dually appointed Vice-Chancellor at the University of Oxford and Dean of Christ Church. He served in these capacities from 1651 to 1657.[3] Through each of these dynamic and substantial posts, Owen maintained a stalwart commitment to biblical and theological fidelity.

Nowhere was that dedication more readily seen than in his pastoral ministry, first at Fordham (1643–1646), then Coggeshall (1646–1651), and finally at Christ Church, Oxford (1651–1660).[4] He also preached every other Sunday at

---

2   Joel Beeke and Randall J. Pederson, *Meet the Puritans* (Grand Rapids: Reformation Heritage, 2007), 455.

3   Carl Trueman, *John Owen: Reformed Catholic, Renaissance Man* (Burlington, VT: Ashgate, 2007), 4.

4   It was during his time at Coggeshall that Owen officially adopted Congregationalist polity. This came as a result of reading John

St. Mary's, where he shared the pulpit with Thomas Goodwin. It was in these congregational settings that Owen taught, wrote, and lived by the constant exercise of sound teaching.

Owen subscribed to the common Puritan notion that each passage must find its interpretation consistent with a more comprehensive biblical and doctrinal understanding. He maintained, 'There is a harmony, an answerableness, and a proportion, in the whole system of faith, or things to be believed. Particular places are so to be interpreted as that they do not break or disturb this order.'[5] This commitment that every biblical text be treated in light of the whole, to the end of informing daily living, served to guard and guide his pastoral teaching ministry.

Doctrine and the Pastor's Life

A strong emphasis on doctrine for use in everyday life was not unique to Owen. In *The Marrow of Theology*, which was the primary required text among Ivy League institutions in Colonial New England, William Ames (1576–1633) said, 'Theology is the doctrine or teaching of living to God.'[6] For Ames, doctrine and ethics were not entirely distinct areas of concern, but rather they were a 'unified system that helped the Christian live a life of genuine piety.'[7] This Puritan notion is in keeping with Paul's writing to both Timothy and Titus. Those Pastoral Epistles are a rich source for discovering why

---

Cotton's *The Keys of the Kingdom of Heaven*.

5   *Works of John Owen*, ed. William H. Goold (1850–1853; repr., Edinburgh: Banner of Truth, 1968), 25:333.

6   William Ames, *The Marrow of Theology* (Grand Rapids: Baker, 1997), 1623.

7   Beeke and Pederson, *Meet the Puritans*, 43.

sound teaching is so very critical to the life of the church, as it influences the life and ministry of the pastor.

First, *formation of the pastor comes through sound doctrine.* Timothy is implored by Paul to 'hold on' to the gospel ('sound words') he heard from the Apostle (2 Tim 1:13). This admonition follows the notion that the pastor's ministry of the Word is itself 'training' and 'nourishing' him in sound doctrine (1 Tim. 4:6). So, believing and teaching sound doctrine are means of further conforming the pastor into the image of Christ and beautifying the church, His bride.

Second, *caution for the pastor comes through sound doctrine.* Those who teach and live in ways that disregard sound or 'healthy teaching' show themselves to be 'sick'. They are not thriving in gospel hope but are spiritually ill (1 Tim. 1:10). Their malady is teaching that is not Christ-centered, and so it cannot lead to godliness (1 Tim. 6:3). As errant teachers masquerade as pastors, with ear-tickling as their objective, the temptation may arise to lay down the stalwart call – to teach sound doctrine and proclaim the excellencies of Christ (2 Tim 4:3). This caution – that false doctrine leads to ungodliness – should ever guard a pastor's teaching.

Third, *instruction from the pastor must be marked by sound doctrine.* In Paul's writing to Titus, he emphasizes sound doctrine as the indelible mark and root of the pastor's life and teaching. Like Timothy, Titus is to be found 'holding fast the faithful word'. This gospel tethering will enable the pastor to both encourage with sound doctrine and reprove those who do not align with the truth (Titus 1:9). He must teach what is 'fitting' for the church to persevere in gospel faith, maintaining unflinching doctrinal 'purity' (Titus 2:1). Even as younger pastors, both Timothy and Titus were to serve as exemplars of dependence on sound doctrine, which is crucial to a life of faith in Christ (1 Tim. 4:12; Titus 2:7).

Doctrine and the Pastor's Duty

In a 1682 ordination sermon entitled 'The Duty of a Pastor,' Owen carefully outlined what is necessary to faithful pastoral ministry.[8] Taking as his text Jeremiah 3:15, he stressed the primacy of the teaching ministry of the church and the pastor.[9] First, the pastor must feed the church through preaching the gospel. In fact, 'One who does not feed his flock is no pastor.'[10] Second, a pastor is to exercise 'continual prayer' over the church.[11] Lastly, a pastor is to 'preserve the truth and doctrine of the gospel that is committed to the church.'[12]

Owen appealed to Paul's words to Timothy to remember that he is to believe and teach the 'glorious gospel of the blessed God', which was entrusted to the Apostle (1 Tim. 1:11, KJV). Paul tells Timothy that this 'good deposit', this treasure of sound doctrine, has now been 'committed to your trust' by 'the Holy Spirit' (1 Tim. 6:20; 2 Tim. 1:14). Owen added,

The church 'is like the tower of David built for an armory, on which there hang a thousand bucklers and shields of mighty men' [Song of Solomon 4:4]. The ministers of the gospel are

---

8   For specific treatment of the emphasis on the pastor's role as preacher, see Matthew Barrett, 'The Duty of a Pastor: John Owen on Feeding the Flock by Diligent Preaching of the Word,' *Themelios* 40, no. 3 (2015): 459–72.

9   Jeremiah 3:15 says, 'And I will give you shepherds after my own heart, who will feed you with knowledge and understanding.'

10   John Owen, 'The Duty of a Pastor,' *Works of John Owen*, 9:453.

11   Chapter 6 of this book interacts with Matthew Henry and the pastoral duty to pray.

12   Owen, 'The Duty of a Pastor,' 458.

shields and bucklers to defend the truth against all adversaries and opposers. The church has had thousands of bucklers and shields of mighty men, or else the truth would have been lost. They are not only to declare it in the preaching of the gospel; but to defend and preserve it against all opposition.[13]

The call to both 'preach' and 'preserve' was then followed by Owen's instructive counsel. He noted four traits of pastors who teach and defend doctrine.

First, *a pastor must possess 'clear apprehension' of sound doctrine.* Owen offered an unsettling reminder: 'Truth may be lost by weakness as well as wickedness.'[14] Our doctrinal conviction and teaching must 'rest upon its own proper grounds and principles', if we hope to defend doctrine against its 'opposers'.[15]

Second, *a pastor must possess 'a love of the truth'*. For Owen, it was essential to know the truth revealed with 'clear apprehension'. However, 'whatever we know of it, unless our love and value of it arise from a sense and experience of it in our own souls,' we will fail to live out what we teach.[16] His estimation of what transpired in his day, among fellow pastors and those who aspired to ministry leadership, sheds light on the present time: 'I fear there is much loss of truth, not for lack of light, knowledge, and ability, but *for lack of love*.'[17]

Next, *a pastor must resist 'novel opinions'*. Owen implored his listeners: 'Let us take heed in ourselves of any inclination to novel opinions, especially in, about, or against such points

---

13 Owen, *ibid.*, 458.

14 Owen, *ibid.*, 459.

15 Owen, *ibid.*, 459.

16 Owen, *ibid.*, 459.

17 Owen, *ibid.*, 459.

of faith as those in which those who have gone before us, and fallen asleep, found life, comfort, and power.'[18] His words then probed the rich inheritance of the Reformation in recapturing justification, redemption, and the perseverance of the saints. The repeated refrain was that 'we have become indifferent' to these grounding truths, and the guard for this occurring is the pastor vigilantly teaching and preserving sound doctrine, for the sake of the congregation. He wrote, 'Bring one man into the congregation who has an opinion, and he will make more stir about it than all the rest of the congregation in building up one another in their most holy faith.'[19]

Finally, *a pastor must possess 'skill and ability' to discern and identify unsound teaching.* Owen mentioned 'prayer, watchfulness, and diligence' as non-negotiable elements of this skill set. He further remarked that those who are 'less skilled would do well to counsel with those who are more experienced', in order to gain further expertise.[20] During this ordination sermon, Owen championed doctrinal precision as a means to joyful perseverance and vigilance in the ministry of teaching.

Doctrine and the Pastor's Communion

As pastors, we desire our teaching to guide our people into sound thinking that will then produce Godward actions. Owen is a worthy example here, as he was concerned with precision in doctrinal conviction and teaching for the expressed purpose of a lived faith. It is not enough to maintain commitment to sound doctrine in proposition. We will not be drawn to depend

---

18   Owen, *ibid.*, 458.

19   Owen, *ibid.*, 460.

20   Owen, *ibid.*, 460.

on God in Christ, 'unless we find the power of the truths abiding in our own hearts and have a continual experience of their necessity and excellency in our standing before God and our communion with Him.'[21]

Among his writings, *Of Communion with God the Father, Son and Holy Ghost* (1657) can serve as a poignant example of this applied focus. In the sermons that were compiled to form *Of Communion*, Owen maintains that our standing before God in Christ is unshakeable, while our experience knowing, loving, and obeying God in Christ can be quite shaky.

We are both in union with Christ and have communion with Christ. Owen notes that this relationship to God is both 'perfect and complete' (union) and 'initial and incomplete' (communion). He writes, 'Our communion, then, with God, consisteth in his communication of himself to us, with our returnal unto him of that which he requireth and accepteth, flowing from that union which in Jesus Christ we have with him.'[22] Our communion with God is a gloriously tangible relationship. He 'communicates' to us and we 'return' love, worship, and obedience to Him. Understanding this dynamic and teaching these truths to others leads to a deeper appreciation of the vibrant relationship God enjoys with His people.[23]

---

21 *Works of John Owen*, 12:52.

22 *Works of John Owen*, 2:8.

23 Kelly Kapic notes the importance of Owen's contrast between union and communion: 'This is an important theological and experiential distinction, for it protects the biblical truth that we are saved by radical and free divine grace. Furthermore, this distinction also protects the biblical truth that the children of God have a relationship with their Lord, and that there are things they can do that either help or hinder it.' Kelly Kapic, 'Introduction: Worshipping the Triune God; The Shape of John Owen's Trinitarian

The Real Task of Ministry

Thinking about our relationship to God, as those who are in Christ and as those who are called to lead congregations to follow Him, can be both breathtaking and terrifying. Looking to the example of a titan like John Owen can have a similar effect. In an attempt to think about the ministries of men like Owen, Sinclair Ferguson observes:

> Here we find ourselves in a world of men with a clear vision of the nature of true pastoral ministry, and an unreserved commitment to it, whatever the personal cost. This is an environment of clear-sightedness, single-mindedness, and a deep love of God which if applied to the work of the pastor today, would have profound, if at times a disturbing impact on our understanding of the real task of ministry.[24]

Although 'disturbing' to an inadequate view of pastoral ministry, a brief look at Owen can help clear away murky and overwhelming ideas about our vocation. The task of pastoral ministry, at its core, is teaching sound doctrine. The vehicles of this ministry are varied. We teach and exhort through counseling. We teach and instruct through writing. We teach and declare through preaching. The substance of what we teach is fixed; it is the unchanging truth of the gospel.

Spirituality,' in *Communion with the Triune God*, by John Owen, ed. Kelly M. Kapic and Justin Taylor (Wheaton, IL: Crossway, 2007), 21.

24 Sinclair Ferguson, *Some Pastors and Teachers* (Carlisle, PA: Banner of Truth, 2017), 167-68.

Lewis Bayly (c. 1575–1631)

Bishop, Bangor (Wales); Royal Chaplain, London

Primary Work

The Practice of Piety

Mentor

Thomas Bayly

'There can be no true piety without the knowledge of God; nor any good practice without the knowledge of a man's own self.'
(Lewis Bayly)

5.

The Pastor's Piety
with Lewis Bayly[1]

John Bunyan and his wife were so poor when they got married – they lacked a dish and spoon between them. Their meager possessions, however, contained a great treasure. Bunyan's bride owned worn copies of two Puritan classics that she inherited from her father. These two volumes, Lewis Bayly's *The Practice of Piety* and Arthur Dent's *A Plain Man's Pathway to Heaven*, would have a profound impact on her husband, sparking his initial interest in religion and eventually influencing his beloved work, *Pilgrim's Progress*.[2]

Although few are familiar with the two books today, Bunyan's story was not uncommon at the time. *The Practice of Piety*, the more well-known of the two, was one of the most widely-

---

1   Lewis Bayly never sat for a portrait. The image on the previous page is of the Bangor Cathedral, which sits on the site where Bayly preached in his day.

2   For more, see Bunyan's spiritual autobiography: John Bunyan, *Grace Abounding to the Chief of Sinners* (1666). Arthur Dent's *A Plain Man's Pathway to Heaven* was first published in 1601; Lewis Bayly's *The Practice of Piety* in 1611.

read books in the English language during the seventeenth century. It was influential in the development of the Puritan concept of piety and, in many ways, piety was the essential element of Puritanism itself. Scholars have variously described Puritanism as 'a devotional movement rooted in religious experience,'[3] a 'spiritual movement, passionately concerned with God and godliness,'[4] and a 'quest for a life reformed by the Word of God'.[5] The Puritans were serious about the business of applying the Bible to everyday life and, as such, their writings provide an excellent lens for helping pastors evaluate their own commitment to the Lord. *The Practice of Piety* demonstrates how the Puritans pursued holiness and challenges pastors today to do the same.

The Ministry and Impact of Lewis Bayly

More is known about Lewis Bayly's famous work than the author himself, but the scant biographical details available reveal that his pastoral ministry was marked by Puritan principles. He was born around 1575 in a minister's home in Wales, where his father served as the curate at Carmarthen. After a brief stint as a grammar school headmaster and then as a pastor in two Worcestershire parishes, Bayly became a royal chaplain to Prince Henry during the first decade of King James' reign. By 1616, he was promoted to the king's chaplain and eventually assigned to the bishopric of Bangor, a small Welsh

---

3   Charles Hambrick-Stowe, preface to *The Practice of Piety: Puritan Devotional Disciplines in Seventeenth-Century New England* (Chapel Hill: University of North Carolina, 1982), vii.

4   J. I. Packer, *A Quest for Godliness: The Puritan Vision for the Christian Life* (Wheaton, IL: Crossway, 1990), 28.

5   Joel R. Beeke and Mark Jones, *A Puritan Theology: Doctrine for Life* (Grand Rapids: Reformation Heritage, 2012), 5.

village originally constructed around a monastic settlement in the sixth century. Bayly would spend the final fifteen years of his life in this post. Though his Puritan sentiments sparked a few minor controversies with church leadership, Bayly remained in the Church of England. He was survived by his second wife – his first wife having died in 1608 – in addition to four sons.

Although relatively unknown today, *The Practice of Piety* was once a staple Protestant devotional. Originally published as a collection of sermons in 1611, Bayly later expanded the work and dedicated the amplified version to Prince Charles of Wales, whose eventual reign as king would be engulfed in civil war. This version was reprinted in over seventy editions within the next two centuries, becoming a fixture in many homes throughout England. Richard Baxter numbered it among the practical works that every young minister should seek to obtain.[6] It was esteemed abroad as well, being translated into several European languages and eventually made available to the Massachusetts Indians in their native tongue. Bayly's work was instrumental in the conversion of the Scotsman James Fraser of Brea (1638–1693) and central to his walk with the Lord. In France, it was so popular that one minister complained his congregation viewed it as equal in authority to the Bible![7] *The Practice of Piety* supplied a model for spiritual devotion throughout the Puritan period and provides a helpful window into Puritan spirituality.

---

6   *Practical Works of Richard Baxter* (London: George Virtue, 1838), 1:732.

7   C. Matthew McMahon and Therese B. McMahon, foreword to *The Practice of Piety*, by Lewis Bayly (1611; repr., Coconut Creek, FL: Puritan Pub., 2012), 17.

The Practice of Piety

As the subtitle makes clear, *The Practice of Piety* aims at 'directing a Christian how to walk that he may please God'. The work begins with a lengthy meditation on the person of God followed by reflections on the miserable difficulties of the irreligious contrasted with the blessings enjoyed by the righteous. This foray into theology proper may seem out of place in a book on Christian living but, as the author notes, 'There can be no true piety without the knowledge of God; nor any good practice without the knowledge of a man's own self.'[8] This notion sets the Puritan approach to piety apart from modern works that emphasize spiritual practices to the neglect of theological foundations. The Puritans recognized the danger of divorcing spirituality from theology and rooted their vision for the Christian life in what Calvin referred to as the double knowledge of God and self. To the modern reader, Bayly's seventy-five-page theological reflection may seem superfluous; to the Puritan, it was essential to genuine piety.

If the demons indeed rejoice over modern connotations of the term 'Puritanism' – as C. S. Lewis famously suggested – they must be equally pleased with the negative overtones surrounding the word *piety*. In contemporary vernacular, this term is often associated with a kind of outward formalism that falls short of wholehearted obedience. People who are overly scrupulous about mundane details are accused of being *pious*, rather than earnest. The Puritans knew nothing of this distinction. Piety was their term for godly living, marked by consistent commitment to biblical convictions. It included both right doctrine and right living, proper action rooted in

---

8   Lewis Bayly, *The Practice of Piety: Directing a Christian How to Walk that he May Please God* (London: Philip Chetwinde, 1692), 2.

appropriate motivation. While expressions of piety could be as varied as individuals themselves, Jerald Brauer notes, 'When Puritans used the term piety, they knew exactly to what they referred.'[9] Piety encompassed the full expression of a person's religion and served as a litmus of its veracity. In many ways, Bayly set the parameters for this concept with his influential work near the beginning of the Puritan movement.

Bayly understood piety to be the dynamic outworking of salvation. It is an expression of progress in sanctification, not a means of securing justification. Like most Puritans, Bayly was a Calvinist who emphasized the sovereignty of God in salvation. The Puritans recognized that the effects of the fall render man incapable of earning God's favor. Neither the church's sacraments nor a person's good works are sufficient to bridge the chasm between a sinful man and a holy God. God Himself must initiate reconciliation through divine election. However, once a person is saved by grace, the Spirit transforms him, bearing fruit in the form of practical godliness. Piety, then, is positive evidence that grace is at work. As Bayly urged his reader, 'If you are desirous to purchase sound assurance of salvation to your soul, and to go the right and safe way to heaven, get forthwith, like a wise virgin (Matt. 25:1), the oil of piety in [your] lamp.'[10] Piety is the price for assurance, but salvation itself was purchased by the cross of Christ.

Bayly's approach to the Christian life is encapsulated in a chart he included in the original edition. The chart neatly summarized the main thesis of the book: the practice of piety consists in (1) knowing God and self; and (2) in glorifying

---

9   Jerald C. Brauer, 'Types of Puritan Piety,' *Church History* 56, no. 1 (March 1987): 39.

10   Bayly, *ibid.*, 107.

God in life and death.[11] A person glorifies God with their life by dedicating themselves to serving Him in both private devotion and public piety. Nearly half of the book focused on expounding this point. Bayly provided detailed instructions and numerous examples to guide his reader on subjects such as Bible study, prayer, meditation, the Sabbath, communion, fasting, feasting, and family worship. Such were the means of grace which the Puritans rightly recognized as central to the pursuit of piety.

The final section of the book is concerned with helping the godly endure sickness and prepare for death. Though less common by the seventeenth century, handbooks devoted to 'the art of dying' (*ars moriendi*) were prevalent throughout the Middle Ages. Far from an afterthought, Bayly devoted nearly a third of his book to the subject, demonstrating that a truly pious life leads to a godly death. The devout Christian must learn to glorify God by dying in the Lord and, if necessary, for the Lord (as a martyr). Among the many helpful sections of this work, one chapter that aimed at examining those obstacles that hinder the pursuit of piety deserves attention.

Hindrances to Piety

Today's pastors face some challenges unique to the modern world, but upon reading Bayly's list of obstacles, it becomes clear that many difficulties persist from age to age. He identified seven such hindrances, beginning with willful ignorance of the truth. As the experienced pastor observed, many individuals seek to justify their lack of godliness by twisting the meaning of certain passages or doctrines. Such 'carnal professors' demonstrate their lack of grace by seeking a path around true

---

11 Bayly, *ibid.*, 1.

repentance. Pointing to passages such as 'Christ Jesus came into the world to save sinners' (1 Tim. 1:15) and 'The blood of Jesus Christ cleanses us from all sin' (1 John 1:7), they claim that calls for piety undermine the sufficiency of Jesus' death.[12] Without dismissing any of the passages – he cites ten in particular and references many more – Bayly exposes each misinterpretation with Scripture, demonstrating that the call to salvation is also a call to pursue holiness. It is true, Bayly concedes, that the grace of God is greater than our sin, but the 'grace of God that bringeth salvation hath appeared to all men, teaching us that, denying ungodliness and worldly lusts, we should live soberly, righteously, and godly, in this present world' (Titus 2:11-12, KJV). Piety necessarily follows grace, yet as Bayly notes, no passage 'promises any grace to any but the penitent heart'.[13]

Similarly, Bayly chastises any who would misapply doctrines, such as justification, election, or freewill, in an attempt to vindicate their sin. He answers each objection with a deft response that demonstrates his expertise of the human heart. It is not difficult to imagine Bayly applying his arguments to his parishioners as he shepherded them toward practical godliness. While pastors may be less likely than others to fall into doctrinal error, they are just as likely to be led astray by their own heart. Bayly's clever exposure of misinformation is helpful for pastors to consider. For example, he warns of the danger of 'adorning vices with the names of virtues'.[14] In every age, Christians must be on guard against the temptation to call 'drunken carousing, drinking of health; spilling of

---

12 Bayly, quoted from the 1599 Geneva Bible.

13 Bayly, *ibid.*, 84.

14 Bayly, *ibid.*, 91.

innocent blood, valor; wrath, hastiness; [and] ribaldry, mirth.'[15] Similarly, Christians should be wary of any who aim to obfuscate in the other direction, labeling 'sobriety in words and actions, hypocrisy; devotion, superstition; zeal in religion, Puritanism.'[16] As Bayly makes clear, the sinful heart will seek any means possible to justify its actions. He concludes, 'And while thus we call evil good and good evil, true piety is much hindered in her progress.'[17]

A second hindrance of piety is the example of successful people who seem to advance in life despite their ungodliness. Observing that many of the most well-regarded men in his day paid little attention to religion, Bayly warned his reader not to be led astray by their example. Of course, this temptation is as much of a challenge today as it was in the seventeenth century. The human heart longs for recognition and scoffs at obscurity. Holiness can feel like an obstacle in the pursuit of worldly ambitions. For this reason, pastors must reject the allure of popularity and look to Christ as their ultimate example. The path to worldly achievement will rarely cross through Golgotha. The way of the godless will never ultimately please the Lord. As Bayly warns, 'Let not the example of irreligious great men hinder your repentance.'[18]

Others may be hindered in their pursuit of piety by presuming on the patience or mercy of God. In both instances, unrepentant individuals mistake the grace of God for a guarantee that their own sin will be pardoned. Such a conclusion leads to complacency. Pastors may find themselves facing a

---

15   Bayly, *ibid.*, 91.

16   Bayly, *ibid.*, 91.

17   Bayly, *ibid.*, 91.

18   Bayly, *ibid.*, 93.

similar temptation as they labor each week to proclaim the mercies of God. Reminding others of God's grace for sinners could lead a minister to think lightly of his own sin. Again and again, pastors must preach the gospel to their people and to themselves, holding in tension the awesome holiness of God as well as His relentless love. Reflecting on the thief who received mercy in his final hour, Bayly strikes this balance admirably: 'God spared the thief but not his fellow. God spared one, that no man might despair; [yet] God spared but one that no man should presume.'[19]

For others, social relations may serve as obstacles to piety. Bayly warns against keeping too much company with godless men, whom he calls 'the devil's chief instruments'.[20] Too many Christians are led astray by ungodly friends, who either convince them to follow their course into unrighteousness or scoff at their efforts to honor God. Bayly warns his reader, 'Let not the company of earthly sinners hinder you from the society of heavenly saints!'[21] Bayly is to be commended for his passion for holiness, but his strong condemnation of the ungodly seems to leave little room for personal evangelism. It is true that such company can corrupt, but Christians must balance this danger with the call to love their neighbor. Finding the balance between being in the world but not of it is something that every pastor must learn and model for his people.

The final hindrance to piety Bayly noted was the false impression many carry that they will enjoy a long life. Death is sure to come to all and to some long before they expect it. 'The longest life here,' he reasons, 'when it comes to the end, will

---

19   Bayly, *ibid.*, 95.

20   Bayly, *ibid.*, 96.

21   Bayly, *ibid.*, 97.

appear to have been just as a tale that is told, a vanishing vapor, a flitting shadow, a seeming dream, a glorious flower, growing and flourishing in the morning, but in the evening cut down and withered.'[22] This somber acknowledgment should inspire one to repent of all indolence and to pursue holiness 'without which no one will see the Lord' (Heb. 12:14).

Keep Watch Over Your Soul

If this is the Puritan vision for all Christians, how much more should it inspire pastors entrusted with the responsibility to lead others? Pastor, your piety matters to your church. You know this, of course, but does your regular schedule reflect it? When you allocate time and energy toward the spiritual disciplines, do you do so with a view toward what is at stake? Are you a model of piety for your people? A brilliant sermon can be silenced by a lifestyle that contradicts it. As a leader, you must strive 'to keep the commandment unstained' (1 Tim. 6:14), so that 'the word of God may not be reviled' (Titus 2:5). You are a steward of the mysteries of God (Col. 1:24–25), and someday you will give an account for the way in which you have kept watch over the souls entrusted to your care, including your own (Heb. 13:17).

The author of Hebrews exhorts pastors to anticipate this future reckoning with joy rather than fear. Ministers should delight in the responsibility instead of dreading future judgment. One fears the consequences while the other takes pleasure in the privilege. One views ministry as a set of tasks to perform – a means of self-justification, aimed at productivity and accomplishment; the other recognizes it as a sacred trust. One is founded on the pastor's relationship to his work, the

---

22 Bayly, *ibid.*, 103.

other rests on his relationship with God. The key difference may be the pastor's ability to continually think of himself first and foremost as a follower of Christ.

If pastors are keeping watch over the souls of others, they surely must scrutinize their own. The Puritans took this call to vigilance seriously and recognized its importance in the Christian life. A central question permeated the concept of Puritan piety: How can one be certain he is in good standing with the Lord? Holiness in life and death was not considered a means of earning salvation but the biblical path to joyous assurance.

Matthew Henry (1662–1714)

Pastor in Chester and Hackney, England

Primary Works

A Method for Prayer
Commentary on the Whole Bible

Mentors

Philip Henry (1631–1696), Richard Steele (1629–1692)

'God's grace can save souls without preaching, but our preaching cannot save them without God's grace, and that grace must be sought by prayer.' (Matthew Henry)

6.

The Pastor's Prayers
with Matthew Henry

If a modern pastor looks at his calendar and workflow, John Bunyan's famed words may prove hard to hear: 'You can do more than pray after you have prayed, but you cannot do more than pray until you have prayed. Pray often, for prayer is a shield to the soul, a sacrifice to God, and a scourge to Satan.'[1] Bunyan provides a blunt reminder that our days are often flimsily supported by brief, inconsistent petitions. We know that the hours should be marked by consistent prayer, but how might we recapture Bunyan's foundational commitment to pray 'often' in order to benefit from this 'shield' and make this 'sacrifice' with joy? How can we become pastors who are guided by a genuine spirit of prayer? Following the Puritan example in general, and Matthew Henry specifically, might move us to share their noted devotion to prayer.

Matthew Henry: Imitating a Prayerful Pastor

Expelled from the Church of England in 1662, Philip Henry (1631–1696) was still reeling from the repercussions of the Act

---

1   John Bunyan, *Prayer* (Carlisle, PA: Banner of Truth, 1999), 23.

of Uniformity. In that same year his son Matthew was born. Philip's son would grow from a premature infant, to a hearty soul, known for piety and joy. These formative steps followed a path through pastorates in Chester and Hackney.

While he is commonly remembered as a Bible commentator, Matthew Henry's life and writings are perhaps most explicitly concerned with practical piety. In addition to his six-volume *Commentary on the Whole Bible*, he penned over thirty additional writings. Among these contributions are such practical works as *The Pleasantness of a Religious Life*, *The Secret of Communion with God*, *The Young Christian*, and *A Method for Prayer*. His *Method for Prayer* expressed in print the essence of Henry as a 'prayerful pastor'.[2]

A Trusted Method for Prayer

Henry saw the centrality of prayer as a guiding light that most fully shone when prayers were dually shaped in *theological form* and *biblical focus*. Therefore, his method provides a sequential outline for prayer: adoration, confession, petition, thanksgiving, intercession, and conclusion. For Henry, this sequence had to bear the substance of biblical fidelity and language.[3]

Since the Bible is 'perfectly fitted for the end for which it was designed', Henry's method for prayer proceeds from this

---

2   Allan Harman, *Matthew Henry: His Life and Influence* (Fearn, Scotland: Christian Focus, 2012), 179.

3   Henry's pastoral approach and proposed model of prayer is aptly described by William Gurnall (1617–1679), speaking of Christians in general: 'The mightier any is in the Word, the more mighty he will be in prayer' (William Gurnall, *The Christian in Complete Armour* [Edinburgh: Banner of Truth, 2002], 2:420-21).

foundation.[4] Hughes Oliphant Old observes, 'What interested Henry was what Scripture has to say that will direct us in how we are to glorify God and enjoy him forever.'[5] Prayer that is rooted in Scripture and 'methodically' organized can help us to more earnestly pray for those around us.

Henry also makes clear at the outset of his work that the sequence ('method') that he outlines is not rigidly prescriptive and inflexible. It is not to be viewed as a tight playbook from which the readers dare not deviate:

And though I have here recommended a good method for prayer, and that which has been generally approved, yet I am far from thinking we should always tie ourselves to it; that may be varied as well as the expression. Thanksgiving may very aptly be put sometimes before confession or petition, or our intercessions for others before our petitions for ourselves, as in the Lord's Prayer. Sometimes one of these parts of prayer may be enlarged upon much more than another; or they may be decently interwoven in some other method.[6]

What is most significant to Henry is the rightful place of the heart and mind:

But after all, the intention and close application of the mind, the lively exercises of Faith and Love, and the outgoings of holy desire towards God, are so essentially necessary to Prayer, that

---

4   Matthew Henry, *An Exposition of the Old and New Testaments*, Vol. 3 (London: Joseph Robinson, 1839), 302.

5   Hughes Oliphant Old, 'Matthew Henry,' in *Historical Handbook of Major Biblical Interpreters*, ed. Donald McKim (Downers Grove, IL: InterVarsity Press, 1998), 198.

6   Matthew Henry, *A Method for Prayer*, J. Ligon Duncan, III, rev. ed. (Fearn, Scotland: Christian Heritage, 2015), 15.

without these in sincerity, the best and most proper language is but a lifeless image.... Thus therefore we ought to approve ourselves to God in the integrity of our hearts, whether we pray by, or without a pre-composed Form.[7]

The method proposed by Henry provides outlined guidance for both private and public prayers, to be used not in robotic adherence, but with thankful redirection. As we pray personally (privately) and lead others in prayer (publicly), Henry's 'Method' can instruct the form and substance.

The Pastor and the Discipline of Private Prayer

In *The Secret Key to Heaven*, Thomas Brooks (1608–1680) outlines his reasons for writing a work on 'private' or 'closet' prayer. Among these motives, he maintains that 'The power of religion and godliness lives, thrives, or dies, as closet prayer lives, thrives, or dies. Godliness never rises to a higher pitch than when men keep closest to their closets.'[8] Similarly, constancy in private prayer, in Henry's estimation, should move us to begin, maintain, and end each day with prayer.[9]

Matthew's father, Philip, had a knack for creatively summarizing truths that would aid in this type of daily

---

7   Henry, *ibid.*, 16.

8   Thomas Brooks, preface to *The Secret Key to Heaven* (Carlisle, PA: Banner of Truth, 2006), xiv.

9   In the updated edition, edited by Duncan, the book is divided into two parts, the first containing Henry's *A Method for Prayer* in its entirety; the second section offers three sermons on prayer from the Psalms, with each one addressing a time for the daily practice of prayer (morning, throughout the day, and in the evening). Additional works which offer help for the practice of daily private prayer are Samuel Lee's *Secret Prayer Successfully Managed*, Nathaniel Vincent's *The Spirit of Prayer*, and Isaac Watts' *A Guide to Prayer*.

devotion, often arranging these ideas into alphabetical lists. One such list features an 'A-Z' response to the question 'What is prayer?' The letter 'K' entry reads 'Key, to unlock all our treasure.'[10] This line then bears an asterisk. The associated note reads 'Though prayer be the key to open God's treasures, yet faith is the hand that turns the key, without which it will do no good.'[11]

Reflecting on 1 Thessalonians 5:17, John Preston argues that the command to 'pray continually' should *minimally* lead us to pray 'twice a day, morning and evening.' Of this consistency in prayer, he asks:

> Moreover, do our hearts not need it? Are they not ready to go out of order? Are they not ready to contract hardness, are they not ready to go from the Lord and be hardened from God's fear? Therefore, this duty is needful in that regard to compose them and bring them back again into order.[12]

Preston then identifies the range of 'difficulties' that we encounter:

> Again, the variety of occasions hinders us – everything keeps us back. If a man's heart is cheerful, it is apt to delight in other things. If a man's heart is sad, on the other hand, if it is a slight

---

10 Philip Henry 'What is Prayer?' in *Lives of Philip and Matthew Henry*, ed. J. B. Williams (Carlisle, PA: Banner of Truth, 1974), 401.

11 The quote is from a five-message series entitled 'The Saint's Daily Exercise,' delivered by John Preston (1587–1628), who served as Master of Emmanuel College in Cambridge. The collection is considered 'the classic Puritan work on prayer,' among sermons, and it influenced the thinking of both Philip and Matthew Henry. Don Kistler, preface to *The Puritans on Prayer*, by John Preston, ed. Don Kistler (Morgan, PA: Soli Deo Gloria, 1995), iii.

12 Preston, *The Puritans on Prayer*, 14-15.

sadness, men are ready to drive it away with company and sports, with doing other things. And if the sadness is great, we are swallowed up with an anguish of spirit, and then anything is easier than to pray, as you may see by the case of Judas. It was easier to dispatch himself than to go and call upon God. So it is with high men when they have excessive grief, when their anguish of heart is exceeding great. Therefore, whether a man has a cheerful disposition or a sad disposition, whether the sadness is great or small, still you shall find a difficulty.[13]

Because of perennial pastoral stress and lurking tendencies toward ministerial burnout, resiliency in prayer may be best served by precise and honest consideration of our own 'impediments' to consistency. Preston lists three primary areas that hinder prayer: (1) worldly cares and worldly-mindedness; (2) ignorance of the nature of God; and (3) the sins we commit.[14]

Preston's no-nonsense grit is refreshing to pastors leading the church:

But if the impediments are so many, and the difficulties that keep us from a constant course in prayer, and from the performance of it to purpose, are so great, then we must put on a resolution to break through all and lay it as an inviolable law upon ourselves that we will not alter. Let us think to ourselves that the thing is difficult and will cost all the care and all the intention that may be. Yes, when you have overcome the difficulties at one time, it may be, the next day you shall meet with new conflicts, new distempers, new affections, new strength of lust, and a new

---

13   Preston, *ibid.*, 31-32.

14   Preston, *ibid.*, 32-33.

disposition of mind will be on them. And, therefore, he who will be constant in this duty must put on a strong resolution.[15]

This 'resolution' must take on a pattern of 'customary, formal' scheduling and prayer. This consistency of method can then also bolster the practice of public prayer.

The Pastor and the Dimensions of Public Prayer

In keeping with Preston's admonitions, Henry applies a resolute, scripturally-bound approach to the private realm, while he also masterfully crafts an index of example prayers for public life. These entries include, but are not limited to, prayers to be shared between families, offered with the church, and delivered for those in a pastor's community and world.[16]

Pastors pray with the family. In his *Method for Prayer*, Henry outlines prayers for the family in several helpful categories. First, he offers prayers for children, including those based on the Lord's Prayer and his own Catechism.[17] These prayers are noteworthy for both engaging the hearts of parents and communicating in ideas and language appropriate for listening children. Henry strikes a rare balance in crafting model prayers that are doggedly faithful to Scripture and instructive to young hearts and minds.

Providing working models of 'morning' and 'evening' prayer for a family, even specific examples of family petitions for the 'Lord's Day', Henry offers a series of templates for how parents are to pray with, and for, their children. The Godward

---

15 Preston, *ibid.*, 33-34.

16 For further reading on public prayer, see Samuel Miller's *Thoughts on Public Prayer*.

17 Henry, *A Method for Prayer*, 181.

sincerity in his prayers are appreciated by any parent who has known challenging seasons:

> Lord, it is thy good providence that hath built us up into a family, we thank thee for the children thou hast graciously given thy servants; the Lord that hath blessed us with them, make them blessings indeed to us, that we may never be tempted to wish we had been written childless.[18]

Resisting this temptation in his own family, Henry proved to be an exemplary model for those around him, taking joy in praying regularly with his children.[19] The method outlined by Henry was to offer assistance to other fathers and heads of families in leading their family in prayer. His intention was to provide biblically-derived direction for the family to learn and use 'the language of prayer' by means of imitation.[20]

Pastors pray with the church. Since prayer in the corporate worship setting is a means of pastoral leadership, how we pray – word choice, order, tone, spirit – must also be guided by scriptural immersion. Henry maintained that the Bible must be the ground for prayer, to guard from repetition, shallowness, or lopsided emphases in our confession or petition.

Henry includes a prayer that might occur at the beginning of 'public worship', for the 'master of the assemblies', which would weekly take place on the Lord's Day.[21] Prayers accompanying other pastoral responsibilities are outlined by Henry, including

---

18 Henry, *ibid.*, 183.

19 Henry's own method was based, in part, on the prayer outlined in the Westminster Assembly's *Directory of Worship*.

20 Old, 'Matthew Henry,' 77.

21 Henry, *A Method for Prayer*, 125-26.

before, during, and after celebrating the Lord's Supper.[22] He offers examples of how we might lead in prayer on specific occasions such as baptisms, weddings, and the ordination of ministers.[23]

While these events are bright and celebratory, Henry also recognizes the very real diet of pastoral ministry that includes bearing the burdens of those we shepherd. In addition to a particularly gospel-saturated funeral prayer, he also offers examples of how we might pray for those who are 'melancholy' and 'under doubts and fears about their spiritual state', along with words uttered for those 'under convictions of sin' as well as 'those who are sick and in Christ comforted'.[24] He teaches us to be precise and exacting in how we pray for those under our care, as he divides the prayers for the ill into short forms: 'if it be the beginning;' 'if it have continued long;' 'if there be hopes of recovery;' or if it is 'at the point of death'.[25] This approach extends to prayers for sick children and families who experience the loss of a loved one. The instruction that we may gain is one of scripturally-rooted words of prayer, aimed precisely at the occasion and those immersed in it, such that the light of the gospel might shine even where it may appear dim for the moment.

Pastors pray for the world. Praying for those around us who are outside of Christ, and praying in general for our neighborhood, state, nation and world, can be overwhelming. Henry's examples provide helpful categories, while also

---

22 Henry, *ibid.*, 127-28.

23 Henry, *ibid.*, 128-29.

24 Henry, *ibid.*, 128-31.

25 Henry, *ibid.*, 132-34.

demonstrating how God's Word should come to bear on our concerns for the world around us.

Among the model prayers are those that encompass global mission concerns including the conversion of 'the lost world'; specific prayers for the conversion of the Jews; the 'enlargement of the church'; and the naming of 'atheists' and 'deists' as those we desire to see brought to faith.[26] Henry intercedes for his own nation and others, praying specifically for 'continuance of our outward peace', 'the healing of unhappy divisions,' the character and work of politicians, public servants and even heads of state.[27] He pleads for the 'suppression of vice', and for 'our enemies', placing at the center of all of these petitions the gospel hope as offered in the Scripture.[28] He prays for his community and nation: 'Let us never know what a famine of the word means; nor ever be put to wander from sea to sea, and from the river to the ends of the earth, to seek the word of God.'[29]

The Determined Resolve to be a Man of Prayer

How do we heed Henry's example so that we are more constant in prayer? First, *a pastor must make prayer a discipline practiced throughout each day*. Scheduling prayer does not strip it of grace. For Henry and Preston, it is evidence of God's grace that we both have the means for prayer and that we would make it a priority to build our calendars around rather than to rely on spontaneity alone in cultivating prayerful dependence on Christ.

---

26   Henry, *ibid.*, 103-07.

27   Henry, *ibid.*, 108-14.

28   Henry, *ibid.*, 108-10.

29   Henry, *ibid.*, 110.

Second, *a pastor must understand that obstacles to this discipline, whether light or severe, will always be a challenge.* Strained schedules, sick kids, unforeseen staff transitions – the variety of impediments to daily prayer seem unending. Pastors must rest in God's providence. This pressure is normal, and it is the very reason that constancy in prayer must meet these difficulties head-on.

Third, *a pastor must address root causes for why these obstacles keep us from prayer.* The normalcy of obstacles to prayer is reassuring, but this recognition must lead us to look underneath these 'impediments' to the foundational malady. Is our 'worldly-mindedness' and 'care', as Preston put it, maintaining a grip on our time, resources, and perspective on ministry such that we cannot see the way to prayer? Is it the case that we have forgotten the nature of God, so that we do not see clearly on whom we ought to depend, or how He might respond to our needs? Finally, are we coddling and enabling our sin, so that its ripples find their way into the unfolding of the day and drench the hours that might otherwise be marked by devotion to God in private and public prayer?

Fourth, *a pastor must exercise determined resolve, if he will be sustained by prayer.* Michael Haykin notes the depth of understanding displayed by the Puritans, as to the condition of the regenerate human heart, which can still have 'an allergic reaction' to God's presence.[30] This tendency is why we must be resolute, in unqualified dependence on the Holy Spirit, to persist in prayer. Even John Bunyan knew the difficulties of praying consistently:

---

30 Michael Haykin, *The Reformers and Puritans as Spiritual Mentors* (Kitchener, Ontario: Joshua Press, 2012), 172.

For, as for my heart, when I go to pray, I find it so loath to go to God, and when it is with him, so loath to stay with him, that many times I am forced in my Prayers, first to beg God that he would take mine heart, and set it on himself in Christ, and when it is there, that he would keep it there (Ps. 86:11). Nay, many times I know not what to pray for, I am so blind, nor how to pray, I am so ignorant; only (blessed be Grace) the Spirit helps our infirmities (Rom. 8:26).[31]

Praying with constancy, as we invest in private prayer, must also be wedded to our pastoral responsibilities to pray with and for others. May the simple commemoration that Hughes Oliphant Old so beautifully remarked about Henry be true of us in the end: 'He was a minister of the Word and a man of prayer.'[32]

---

31 Richard Greaves, ed., *The Miscellaneous Works of John Bunyan*, vol. 2, *The Doctrine of the Law and Grace unfolded and I will pray with the Spirit* (Oxford: Oxford University Press, 1976), 256-57.

32 Hughes Oliphant Old, 'Matthew Henry and the Discipline of Family Prayer,' in *Calvin Studies VII*, ed. John Leith (Davidson, NC: Colloquium on Calvin Studies, 1994), 69.

7.

The Pastor's Family
with William Gouge

As evidenced by the negative remarks quoted in chapter one, critics have long accused the Puritans of being overly scrupulous and unnecessarily serious. Their reputation as religious prudes would suggest their writings to be a barren source for advice on marriage and family. However, many Puritans devoted whole treatises to these subjects, approaching them with the same biblical precision they brought to bear on other topics. Their serious reflections on the issues of marriage and family prove to be theologically-rich and spiritually-encouraging.

Their homes were characterized by order and discipline, aimed at instilling what they considered to be biblical principles. Puritan pastors instructed their congregants on family life, endeavored to set a godly example in their own homes, and composed several works on the subject. The most influential family handbook written by a Puritan was *Of Domestical Duties* (1622) by William Gouge, a renowned preacher regarded as one of the ablest theological minds of his generation. Gouge pastored the Blackfriars congregation of London for over forty-five years and helped author the *Westminster Confession of Faith* (1646). As a devoted husband to his wife, Elizabeth (1586–1625), and father to thirteen children, Gouge wrote from both pastoral as well as personal experience.

Of Domestical Duties offers a meticulous exegesis of Ephesians 5:21–6:4, rooted in an extended survey of Christ's relationship with his Church. This emphasis makes a profound point: the gospel is the necessary foundation for building a godly home. Much of the work addresses the individual duties of each spouse, beginning with the wife's call to respect her husband and then moving on to the husband's responsibility to exercise loving authority over his wife. As Gouge works through the mutual duties of husbands and wives, he examines sexual faithfulness, love, mutual help in the home, and care for one another's souls, health, reputation, and property. For each admonition, the Puritan pastor offers detailed advice on how spouses fulfill their biblical responsibility to one another as well as warnings about how they may depart from faithfulness. Over the course of this seven-hundred-page tome, several key lessons emerge as most instructive for families today.

The Significance of the Home

The home, according to the *Westminster Confession of Faith* is 'the seminary of the church and state'.[1] As Gouge related, family life holds substantial implications for society at large: 'Besides, a family is a little church, and a little nation, or at least a lively representation of these.... It is as a school wherein the first principles and grounds of government and subjection are learned, and by which men are fitted to greater matters

---

1   'Mr. Thomas Manton's Epistle to the Reader,' in *Westminster Confession of Faith* (1646; repr., Glasgow: Free Presbyterian Pub., 2003), 9.

in church or nation.'[2] When Gouge challenged his church to build gospel-centered homes, he was seeking to do more than shape individual families. He was also building the nation for the future.

Pastors do well to set these implications before their people today. The private nature of family life can cause parents to feel as if their oft-repeated instructions and unseen sacrifices are insignificant to the world at large. By contrast, Gouge recognized that parents who train their children in the ways of the Lord are both a blessing to their children and to future generations.

The Purposes of Marriage

Since the fourth century, the church has generally recognized Augustine's triad of primary purposes for marriage: procreation, fidelity, and unity. The African bishop's order was considered significant; marriage is first and foremost for producing children, then a means of promoting sexual faithfulness, and finally, a relational bond. Many of the Puritans rearranged these ends to place a greater emphasis on mutual companionship. Thomas Gataker (1574–1654), for example, highlighted the logic of recognizing companionship as the primary purpose of marriage: 'If children be a blessing, then the root [from] whence they spring ought to be even more esteemed.... Children are the gift of God, but the Wife is a more

---

2   William Gouge, *Building a Godly Home*, vol. 1, *A Holy Vision for Family Life*, ed. Scott Brown and Joel R. Beeke (1622; repr., Grand Rapids: Reformation Heritage, 2013), 20. This edition of Gouge's classic has been updated and modernized from the original text into three separately-titled volumes.

special gift of God.'[3] Although Gouge retained the traditional order when listing the purposes, he articulated a similar high view of companionship:

Husband and wife [should] be a mutual help to one another, a help as for bringing forth, so for bringing up children, and as for starting, so for well governing their family. A spouse is a help also for managing prosperity well, and bearing adversity well; a help in health and sickness; a help while both live together, and when one is by death taken from the other.[4]

This mutuality is to be rooted in genuine love for one another. Gouge was wise (and ahead of his time) to recognize that genuine friendship works like glue to hold a marriage together: 'If at first there is a good liking mutually and thoroughly settled in both their hearts for one another, love is likely to continue in them forever.'[5] With friendship adhering spouses to one another, Gouge counseled couples to look to the love of Christ as the model.

Pastors must labor to keep this picture of biblical, selfless love before their people, lest the notions of a godless culture creep into their thinking on the subject. Here, Gouge is as helpful as any modern author in describing true love:

In imitation of Christ husbands should love their wives, even if there is nothing in wives to move them so to do, but only because they are their wives.... True love gives its attention to the person

---

3   Thomas Gataker, *A Good Wife God's Gift* (London: John Haviland, 1623), 11.

4   William Gouge, *Building a Godly Home*, vol. 2, *A Holy Vision for a Happy Marriage*, ed. Scott Brown and Joel R. Beeke (1622; repr., Grand Rapids: Reformation Heritage), 30.

5   Gouge, *Holy Vision for Happy Marriage*, 18.

which is loved, and the good love may do to her, rather than to the person who loves, and the good that he may receive.[6]

Healthy Intimacy

Reordering the ends of marriage underscored the importance of affection, and specifically sexual intimacy, in marriage. Although the Puritans have long been categorized as prudish killjoys, their discussions of sexuality tended to be frank and, in their own way, positive. Modern caricatures have ignored passages such as the following from Gouge, which detailed the necessity of couples granting 'due benevolence' to one another (a euphemism for sexual relations taken from the Authorized Version rendering of 1 Corinthians 7:3):

> One of the best remedies [against adultery] that can be prescribed to married persons is that husband and wife mutually delight in each other, and maintain a pure and fervent love between themselves, yielding that due benevolence to one another which is authorized and sanctified by God's Word, and ordained of God for this particular purpose. This 'due benevolence' (as the Apostle calls it in 1 Corinthians 7:3) is one of the most proper and essential acts of marriage. It is necessary for the main and principal ends of it: as for preservation of chastity in those who have not the gift of sexual self-control for celibacy, for increasing the world with legitimate offspring, and for linking the affections of the married couple more firmly together. These ends of marriage, at least the former two, are made void without this duty being performed. As it is called 'benevolence' because it must be performed with good will and delight, willingly, readily

---

6   Gouge, *ibid.*, 260.

and cheerfully; so it is said to be 'due' because it is a debt which the wife owes to her husband, and he to her.[7]

Gouge connected sexuality to each of God's foundational purposes for marriage. Not only is sex necessary for procreation and the satisfaction of desire, it is also a God-given means of cultivating companionship within the marriage. By stirring the couple's affection for one another, sexual intimacy strengthens the bond between husband and wife. It is, therefore, a significant aspect of marriage and ought not to be neglected.

Marriage and Spiritual Growth

The Puritans lived in a time when centuries of clerical celibacy had convinced many that marriage was a hindrance to spirituality. By contrast, Gouge saw the proximity of husband and wife as an opportunity to encourage one another in the Lord. He offered practical advice to this end, instructing spouses to pray together to strengthen their relationship with each other and to fulfill their duties to God. To spur couples on in this endeavor, he listed five items couples should regularly pray for together, including their marital unity, purity, their children, their needed provisions, and their own spiritual development.

For Gouge, each spouse held a responsibility to build up the other:

> There is great need that husbands and wives should work to help advance the growth of grace in each other, because we are all so prone to fall away and grow cold, even as water if the fire go out, and more fuel not be put under it. And of all others, husbands and wives may be most helpful because they can soonest see

---

7   Gouge, *ibid.*, 44.

the beginning of decay by reason of their close and continual familiarity together.[8]

That last point – that the nearness of the husband-wife relationship provided them with an advantage in edifying one another – was of significance to Gouge. He considered it one of the unique blessings of marriage, rooted in God's purpose of mutual companionship. When God gave the woman to man as his helper and entrusted her to him as her provider, the Creator surely intended these responsibilities to include spiritual care. Thus, Gouge counseled couples to think about how they might maximize their relationship for mutual encouragement to the glory of God. This call rings as loud in the present day as it did in the seventeenth century.

Loving Leadership

While the Puritans affirmed that each spouse should seek to build up their mate, they also acknowledged the unique calling of the husband to lead the home. As Gouge noted, the foundation of this call rested on the husband's duty to first lead his wife: 'Though the man be as the head, yet is the woman as the heart, which is the most excellent part of the body next to the head, far more excellent than any other member under the head, and almost equal to the head in many respects, and as necessary.'[9] Gouge called for the centrality of love in all of the husband's actions toward his wife, even those rooted in his authority:

Love is a distinct duty in itself ... which must be joined to every other duty to season and sweeten them. His look, his speech,

---

8   Gouge, *ibid.*, 81.

9   Gouge, *ibid.*, 102.

his conduct, and all his actions, in which he has to do with his wife, must be seasoned with love. Love must show itself in his commandments, in his reproofs, in his instructions, in his admonitions, in his authority, in his familiarity, when they are alone together, when they are in company before others, in civil affairs, in religious matters, at all times, in all things. As salt must be first and last upon the table, and eaten with every bit of meat, so must love be first in a husband's heart, and last out of it, and mixed with everything in which he has to do with his wife.[10]

The emphasis on love was intended to both honor God and create the proper environment in the home. To this end, Gouge argued that 'If a husband carries himself to his wife as God requires, she will find her yoke to be easy, and her submission a great benefit even to herself.'[11] Gouge's point is significant: the responsibilities of wives to joyfully support their husband's leadership and of children to honor their parents are made easier when the home is led well by a loving husband and father.

Training Children in the Lord
Gouge believed that a husband bears responsibility to both lead his wife and provide spiritual direction for his family. He taught men to lead daily worship for those entrusted to their care, to set an example of private devotion, and to guard the purity of their homes. Gouge practiced what he preached in this regard, rising at 4 a.m. each day to read his Bible and pray before leading his family in both morning and evening devotions together.

10   Gouge, *ibid*, 183.

11   Gouge, *ibid.*, 170.

He also encouraged mothers to embrace their own spiritual responsibilities, noting that children often spend more time with their mothers than anyone else, particularly in the early years. So, both parents must recognize their duty to instruct their children. All too often, as Gouge lamented, 'The father's putting off this duty to the mother, and the mother's putting it off to the father is a great cause of the neglect of it.'[12]

Instead, as the following admonition made clear, Gouge's vision for the home involved parents partnering together for the good of their children and the glory of God:

> Let therefore husbands and wives assist one another, for so they may be very helpful to one another, and bring, by their mutual help in governing, much good to the family. The husband by his help aiding his wife, adds much authority to her, and so causes her not to be despised, nor thought little of. The wife by her help causes many things to be discovered, and so fixed, which otherwise might never have been found out. Two eyes see more than one, especially when one of those is more at hand, and more often present, as the wife [often] is in the house.[13]

They Knew How to Love

Thus, the Puritan perspective on marriage and family is far more positive than some might assume. As Edmund Morgan concluded, 'The Puritans were neither prudes nor ascetics. They knew how to laugh and they knew how to love.'[14] Although

---

12 William Gouge, *Building a Godly Home*, vol. 3, *A Holy Vision for Raising Children*, ed. Scott Brown and Joel R. Beeke (1622; repr., Grand Rapids: Reformation Heritage, 2013), 131.

13 Gouge, *Holy Vision for Happy Marriage*, 89.

14 Edmund Morgan, *The Puritan Family: Religion and Domestic Relations in Seventeenth-Century New England* (New York: Harper

they addressed some issues unique to their historical context, much of their reflection on family life remains relevant.

Extending the emphases of the Reformation, the Puritans rejected the veneration of virginity and sought to re-establish the goodness of marriage in the mind of the church. They did so by stressing the role of companionship as a God-given purpose for marriage, a key motivation for affection and intimacy, and even as a foundation for mutual edification. The emphasis on companionship also nuanced their teaching on male headship, providing important caveats for the husband's authority over his wife and home.

Pastors today can learn much from how the Puritans sought to lead their families and how they counseled others to live out biblical principles in the home. They were eager to make the most of day-to-day family interactions. Such moments are so commonplace it can be easy to look past their significance. The Puritans are a helpful corrective to this impulse; they took a serious view toward the family, because they viewed this 'seminary' of church and society as a true seedbed for future generations.

& Row, 1966), 64.

William Perkins (1558–1602)

Lecturer, St. Andrews Church, Cambridge

Teaching Fellow, Christ's College, Cambridge

Primary Work

The Art of Prophesying

Mentor:

Laurence Chaderton (1536–1640)

'The Word of God alone is to be preached, in its perfection and inner consistency. Scripture is the exclusive subject of preaching, the only field in which the preacher is to labor.' (William Perkins)

8

The Pastor's Preaching
with William Perkins

On December 17, 1903, a few miles south of Kitty Hawk, North Carolina, brothers Orville and Wilbur Wright achieved lift off in the world's first manned aircraft. They were the 'first in flight'. Almost any child can tell of the Wright Brothers and what their innovation meant to history, but the name Francesco Lana de Terzi (1631–1687) is obscure and unknown. It was de Terzi, an Italian mathematics and physics professor, who developed the concept of a 'flying ship', which he outlined in his work *Prodromo*. His conceptual invention, and related ideas about manned aircraft, warrant his memorial title as the 'Father of Aeronautics'. He blazed the path that led to the hill in North Carolina, where air travel was born.

William Perkins is rightly recognized as the 'Father of Puritanism'. According to J. I. Packer, through his trailblazing preaching and writing, Perkins 'crystallized and delimited the essence of mainstream Puritan Christianity for the next hundred years'.[1] While his memory is indelibly etched in the marble of the Puritan movement's foundation stones, Baxter, Goodwin, Owen, and Edwards are names that we more readily recognize; however, Perkins provides a sturdy model, particularly in his preaching, for an enduring ministry of the Word.

The Preacher and the Lord: Faithful Devotion

Perkins was born in Warwickshire in 1558. In 1577 he began attending Christ's College, Cambridge and it was there that he met Laurence Chaderton (1536–1640) who became his tutor. The friendship between the two endured until the end of Perkins' life, and the preaching of Chaderton was one means God used to convert Perkins while in Cambridge.

After completing his Masters work in 1584, he assumed both the position of fellow at Christ's College and lecturer at St. Andrews Church. He continued to preach at St. Andrews until his death in 1602. He wrote more than fifty treatises over his ministerial lifetime, and in England his writings ultimately superseded those of John Calvin, Theodore Beza, and Heinrich Bullinger at the end of the sixteenth century. Perkins' ability to write for the church in a clear and compelling manner was unmatched at the time.[2]

Additionally, his ministerial roles in Cambridge tested and affirmed unique gifts in preaching, as his diverse audiences consisted of professional academics, those who lived in Cambridge proper, and others who made their way

---

1   J. I. Packer, *Puritan Portraits* (Fearn, Scotland: Christian Focus, 2012), 132.

2   Stephen Yuille, *Living Blessedly Forever: The Sermon on the Mount and the Puritan Piety of William Perkins* (Grand Rapids: Reformation Heritage, 2012), 1-2.

in from more rural areas. Among this varied congregation, 'His style and subject were accommodated to the capacities of the common people, while, at the same time, the pious scholars heard him with admiration.'[3] His commitment to faithful preaching served well those who gathered to hear his exposition of the Bible.

The Preacher and the Text: Faithful Exposition

The most influential resource on Puritan preaching in both England and New England was Perkins' book, *The Art of Prophesying*. It was first published in English in 1607, five years after his death.[4] It is instructive to note that there were both events and activities associated with the term 'prophesying' in Perkins' era. W. B. Patterson helpfully describes the 'prophesying' events:

> 'Prophesyings' were assemblies or conferences, chiefly of clergymen, that had been held in England in the 1560s and 1570s. At these gatherings, a minister delivered a sermon, and a discussion was subsequently held among those in attendance. The discussion focused on the sermon's form, content, and contemporary relevance. The intention of the prophesyings was to improve the participants' understanding of the scriptures and to provide an example of how a text could be treated in a sermon.[5]

---

3 Thomas Fuller, *The Holy State*, vol. 2 (1642), 89.

4 The work was first published in Latin in 1592, under the title *Prophetica*.

5 W. B. Patterson, *William Perkins and the Making of a Protestant England* (Oxford: Oxford University Press, 2014), 118.

These gatherings were a means of 'clerical education', as those in attendance learned what it meant to minister ever more faithfully the Word of God.

Perkins' treatise aimed at the same objective – to educate pastors. Under the notion of 'prophesying', he stressed two activities that are uniquely to occupy the pastor's schedule: preaching and prayer. He writes, 'There are two parts to prophecy: preaching the Word and public prayer. For the prophet (that is, the minister of the Word) has only two duties. One is preaching the Word, the other is praying to God in the name of the people.'[6]

Through the vehicle of preaching, the pastor explains and applies the Bible to the whole of the congregation. The way in which he goes about the explanation and application is the sermon proper; this message must be understandable to the people, corporately and individually.

'Plain style' preaching was the method that ultimately grew out of Perkin's commitments. As Sinclair Ferguson explains, 'Plain' sermons had three distinct movements: exegetical, doctrinal, and applicational. First, the *exegetical* movement allowed for the preacher to present the biblical passage in its context. Second, the central, *doctrinal* emphasis of the passage 'was explained clearly and concisely'.[7] Lastly, direct *application* was made to the specific hearers. Perkins implored the preachers he influenced to resist the temptation to develop intricate oratory, and instead 'hide human wisdom', while 'demonstrating the Spirit' and his divine work.[8]

---

6   William Perkins, *The Art of Prophesying*, rev. ed. (Carlisle, PA: Banner of Truth, 1996), 7.

7   Sinclair Ferguson, *Some Pastors and Teachers* (Carlisle, PA: Banner of Truth, 2017), 745.

8   Perkins, *ibid.*, 71.

As Ferguson observes about the plain approach, 'Unfolding and applying the text of Scripture in a straightforward and simple, yet vigorous and direct style of speech and manner were its hallmarks.'[9] While both 'unfolding' and 'applying' the text were at the forefront of those preachers making use of the plain approach, application, or 'uses' as they called it, accounted for much of the sermon, issuing from an overwhelming devotion to living out the faith.

The Preacher and the Hearer: Faithful Application

In his masterful text, *Preaching and Preachers*, Martyn Lloyd-Jones acknowledges both the theological inheritance we have received from the Puritans and the need to mindfully minister the Word of God among those currently living in our day:

> The chief fault of the young preacher is to preach to the people as we would like them to be, instead of as they are. This is more or less inevitable. He has been reading biographies of great preachers, or perhaps he has been reading the Puritans, and as a result has a picture in his mind, a kind of ideal picture of what preaching should be. He then proceeds to try to do that himself, forgetting that the people who listened to the Puritans – who sometimes preached for three hours at a time – had been trained to do that in various ways more or less for a century.... If a young preacher of today does not understand this point, and tries to preach as the Puritans preached, and preaches for a couple of hours, he will soon find that he will not have a congregation to preach to. It is vitally important that the preacher should make an assessment of the people to whom he is preaching.[10]

---

9   Ferguson, *Some Pastors and Teachers*, 743.

10   D. Martyn Lloyd-Jones, *Preaching and Preachers* (1971; repr., Grand Rapids: Zondervan, 1971), 144-45.

Preachers can often overlook a significant player in the preparation and delivery of the sermon – the hearer. In Perkins' approach, assessing and understanding the condition and needs of those who listen is of special importance. In *The Art of Prophesying*, he offers seven audience types or 'Categories of Hearers': (1) those who are unbelievers and are both ignorant and unteachable; (2) those who are teachable, but ignorant; (3) those who have knowledge, but have never been humbled; (4) those who have already been humbled; (5) those who already believe; (6) those who have fallen back; and (7) churches with both believers and unbelievers.[11]

The detailed categorization of those who listen to the sermon is to inform how the teacher might most directly apply the text. The spectrum includes everyone from those who are 'unteachable' unbelievers, to those who 'have fallen back', and even notes that the 'typical situation' in the churches was to have both believing and unbelieving people present. Since this is also the case for our worship services today, Perkins reminds the preacher that 'Any doctrine may be expounded to them, either from the law or from the gospel ... this is what the prophets did in their sermons, when they announced judgement and destruction on the wicked, and promised deliverance in the Messiah to those who repented.'[12]

Perkins' pulpit approach was inseparably linked to this brand of shepherding conviction, so that the way in which the preacher might establish the 'status' of the hearers and minister the Word *to* them was to be *with* them. He notes:

> The diagnosis of a person's spiritual status involves investigating whether they are under the law or under grace. In order to

11   Perkins, *ibid.*, 56-63.
12   Perkins, *ibid.*, 62.

clarify this we must probe and question to discover from them whether they are displeased with themselves, because they have displeased God. Do they hate sin as sin? That is the foundation of the repentance that brings salvation. Then, secondly we must ask whether they have or feel in their heart a desire to be reconciled with God. This is the groundwork for a living faith.[13]

Application of the text to the hearer takes two forms, according to Perkins. He calls these two kinds of application *mental* and *practical*.

He writes, 'Mental application is concerned with the mind, and involves either doctrine or reproof (2 Tim. 3:16-17).'[14] Sound doctrinal preaching for Perkins included teaching that would assist the hearer to 'come to a right judgement about what is to be believed', while such preaching may also be applied to 'recover the mind from error'.[15]

In similar fashion, 'Practical application has to do with life-style and behavior and involves instruction and correction.'[16] Perkins emphasized both instruction and correction, for the sake of a lived faith. Application through *instruction* should 'enable us to live well in the context of the family, the state and the church. It involves both encouragement and exhortation (Rom. 15:4).'[17]

The counterpart to instruction is *correction*. This brand of practical application is intended to affect 'lives marked by ungodliness and unrighteousness'.[18] In order to properly bring

13 Perkins, *ibid.*, 61.

14 Perkins, *ibid.*, 64.

15 Perkins, *ibid.*, 64.

16 Perkins, *ibid.*, 65.

17 Perkins, *ibid*, 65.

18 Perkins, *ibid.*, 65.

correction through application, the preacher should be more general, initially, 'without reference to specific circumstances.'[19] If this general correction is not fruitful, Perkins guides the preacher to express the admonishment 'in more detailed ways'. His rich shepherding care, coupled with wise pastoral sensitivity is front and center in the following caution:

> But our expressions of hatred for sin must always be accompanied by an obvious love for the person who has sinned. Whenever possible the minister should include himself in his reproofs. In this way his preaching, teaching and counselling will be expressed in a mild and gentle spirit (cf. Dan. 4:16-19; 1 Cor. 4:6; Gal. 2:15).[20]

The conviction to place the preacher under the authority of God's Word, along with his brothers and sisters in the congregation, underscores Perkins' commitment to application that is appropriate to 'the present experiences and condition of the church'.[21] He even reminds the reader that in his selection of application points he must exercise care, limiting the quantity 'lest those who hear God's Word expounded are overwhelmed by the sheer number of applications'.[22] Perkins' exhortations are a call to careful, pastoral application of the text to the people, by the preacher, for the specific 'experiences and condition of the church'.[23]

---

19   Perkins, *ibid.*, 65.

20   Perkins, *ibid.*, 65.

21   Perkins, *ibid.*, 65.

22   Perkins, *ibid.*, 65.

23   Perkins, *ibid.*, 65.

Minister of the Word: Mind Thy Business

William Perkins stood as a shining example in his generation, and his pulpit influenced the thinking and practice of pulpit ministry in each generation since. His 'plain style' preaching method saw the congregation's lived faith as the purpose of the sermon, and the glory of God through His church as its decisive end.

As John Broadus (1827–1895) stated, 'Preaching is the proclamation of God's message by a chosen personality to meet the needs of humanity.'[24] The pastor is the chosen means to meet those needs – through preaching. So, perhaps the reminder that Perkins had engraved on his study desk might serve as a fitting call to us all: 'Thou art a Minister of the Word: Mind thy Business.'

---

24 John Broadus, *On the Preparation and Delivery of Sermons*, 4th ed. (San Francisco: Harper & Row, 1979), 3.

Richard Sibbes (1577–1635)

Lecturer of Divinity, Gray's Inn of London
Vicar, Holy Trinity Church, Cambridge

Primary Works

The Bruised Reed
The Soul's Conflict

Mentor

Paul Baynes (1573–1617)

*'When we feel ourselves cold in affection and duty, the best
way is to warm ourselves at this fire of Christ's love and mercy.'*
(Richard Sibbes)

9

The Pastor's Affections
with Richard Sibbes

Every pastor knows the feeling. Maybe you've spent too many hours in the office lately. Maybe it's been too long since your last vacation. Maybe the weight of your people's worries has simply become too much for your feeble shoulders to bear. Regardless of the cause, you wonder if you can summon the courage to go on. Where can a pastor find encouragement?

When Martyn Lloyd-Jones encountered such difficulties in the middle of the twentieth century, he looked to a Puritan named Richard Sibbes. Like many before him, Lloyd-Jones realized he had discovered 'an unfailing remedy'. The former physician described Sibbes' impact in medicinal terms:

> The heavenly Doctor Sibbes ... was a balm to my soul at a period in my life when I was overworked and badly overtired, and therefore subject in an unusual manner to the onslaughts of the devil.... His books *The Bruised Reed* and *The Soul's Conflict* quieted, soothed, comforted, encouraged, and healed me.[1]

---

1   D. Martyn Lloyd-Jones, *Preaching and Preachers* (1971; repr., Grand Rapids: Zondervan, 1972), 175.

This testimony demonstrates the power of truth tenderly applied. Such preaching not only explains doctrine but also engages the heart. That Sibbes could be effective, despite the historical distance, is evidence of his masterful ability as a physician of the soul. Though few were as gifted as the heavenly Doctor Sibbes at applying the balm of the gospel to weary Christians, his efforts to engage the heart through his preaching are characteristic of the broader Puritan tradition.

The Puritans and Engaging the Heart

The Puritans possessed what J. I. Packer has called 'a minute acquaintance with the human heart'.[2] While historical caricatures tend to emphasize their external scrupulosity, in reality they aimed at the inner person. Stephen Charnock's reflections on Psalm 14:1 ('The fool hath said in his heart, "There is no God"', KJV) are illustrative of how the Puritans understood the operations of the heart. Charnock argued that all sin can be traced back to 'a kind of cursing God in the heart', and that a man's practices betrayed his true inner principles.[3] This functional atheism is rooted in the desire to throw off authority and exalt oneself. Every sin is an act of disordered worship, flowing from an idolatrous heart. As Charnock put it, '"The fool hath said in his heart," and then follows a legion of devils.'[4]

Because the heart is the command center of a person's will, it is the true battleground between sin and righteousness.

---

2   J. I. Packer, *A Quest for Godliness: The Puritan Vision for the Christian Life* (Wheaton, IL: Crossway, 1990), 29.

3   Stephen Charnock, *Discourses upon the Existence and Attributes of God* (1682; repr., Grand Rapids: Baker, 1979), 1:93. Charnock's approach to theology is further discussed in chapter 3.

4   Charnock, *Discourses upon Existence and Attributes of God*, 93.

Before Christ can be rightly worshiped, individuals must destroy the idols of the heart. External improvements are only as effective as they are motivated by inner transformation. Armed with these convictions, Puritan preachers took aim in their sermons, writings, and counseling at the affections. Among his contemporaries, Sibbes stands out as an exemplar of engaging the heart.

The Life and Ministry of Richard Sibbes

As the son of a wheelwright in a small Suffolk village, Sibbes came from humble beginnings. Yet, due to the patronage of benevolent friends, he was able to attend St. John's College at Cambridge, where he was converted under the ministry of the well-known Puritan, Paul Baynes. Baynes worked alongside William Perkins to help transform Cambridge into what has been called a 'Puritan hotbed'.[5] While very few of Baynes' works ever made it into print, a piece of advice attributed to him by William Ames may have influenced Sibbes himself: 'Beware of a strong head and a cold heart.'[6]

Sibbes' time at St. John's exposed him to controversies that would shape the church in his lifetime while rooting him in a confessional Calvinism that provided the foundation for his future ministry. After earning his Bachelor of Divinity in 1610, Sibbes began preaching weekly at Holy Trinity Church in Cambridge before relocating to London in 1617 to become the Lecturer of Divinity at Gray's Inn. He would later return

---

5 This phrase was first used by James Higginson, *Spenser's Shepherd's Calendar in Relation to Contemporary Affairs* (New York: Columbia University Press, 1912), 20.

6 Francis J. Bremer, *The Puritan Experiment: New England Society from Bradford to Edwards*, rev. ed. (Lebanon, NH: University Press of New England, 1995), 42.

to Cambridge when appointed Master of Katherine Hall and, eventually, as vicar of Holy Trinity, but he continued to serve at Gray's Inn for the remainder of his life. These were high-profile posts at the time. His regular addresses to the prestigious legal society were heard by some of the most well-known Londoners of his day. By the time of his death, he possessed, as Mark Dever describes, 'an extensive tree of friendships throughout the London legal, merchant, and clergy communities.'[7] Sibbes remained in the Anglican Church, seeking to effect reform from within, while warning colleagues against the dangers of dissent. As a pastor, his primary instrument was his pulpit, which he wielded with as much passion and affection as any man in his day.

Preaching to the Heart

While Sibbes published very little in his lifetime, some two million words of his sermons have been printed since his death. The seven volumes of his collected works provide an ample window into the tenor of his preaching ministry.[8] In his day, Sibbes was known as 'the honey mouth' or 'the sweet dropper', owing to his winsome way of applying the gospel message to tender consciences. His preaching was said to be so powerful that hardened sinners would avoid his messages for fear of being converted. The testimony of Humphrey Mills is representative of both the style and impact of his preaching. When Mills heard Sibbes for the first time, it was at the end of three years of attempting to quiet his conscience through

---

7   Mark Dever, *Richard Sibbes: Puritanism and Calvinism in Late Elizabethan and Early Stuart England* (Macon, GA: Mercer University Press, 2000), 68.

8   *The Works of Richard Sibbes*, ed. Alexander B. Grosart (1862–1864; repr., Carlisle, PA: Banner of Truth Trust, 1973).

'outward formalities' that only seemed to draw attention to his spiritual failures. In Sibbes, Mills made a happy discovery: 'His sweet soul-melting Gospel-sermons won my heart and refreshed me much, for by him I saw and had much of God and was confident in Christ.'[9] As one contemporary noted, 'Heaven was in him, before he was in heaven.'[10]

Some scholars have labeled Sibbes a mystic but Dever has helpfully demonstrated that the moniker is misleading.[11] Sibbes did not promote the kind of non-rational union-with-God experiences typically associated with the term; in fact, he held a high view of both the intellect and the affections. Ronald Frost explains that 'Sibbes's anthropology held that the mind and the will are merely instruments of the affections', which Dever contends was a particularly good fit for his ecclesiastical and sociopolitical environment.[12] Thus, Dever suggests that Sibbes should be remembered as an 'affectionate theologian' who 'radically interiorized Christianity'.[13]

What is unmistakable about Sibbes' preaching is his emphatic appeals to the heart. He believed that God made

---

9   Referenced in Michael Reeves, foreword to *The Tender Heart*, by Richard Sibbes, Pocket Puritans (1983; repr., Edinburgh: Banner of Truth Trust, 2011), ix.

10 This frequently cited comment was inscribed by Izaak Walton (1593–1683) in his personal copy of one of Sibbes' books.

11 Dever recently updated his monograph on Sibbes into a more accessible introduction that discusses these matters. See Mark Dever, *The Affectionate Theology of Richard Sibbes* (Sanford, FL: Reformation Trust, 2018).

12 Ronald N. Frost, 'The Bruised Reed,' in *The Devoted Life: An Invitation to the Puritan Classics*, ed. Kelly M. Kapic and Randall C. Gleason (Downers Grove, IL: InterVarsity Press, 2004), 89. Also, Dever, *Richard Sibbes*, 160.

13 Dever, *Richard Sibbes*, 157.

Himself known to the mind by coming near to the heart. He spoke often of the unparalleled love of God toward His people, readily adopting sensuous language to make his point. In his own words, he believed that 'the putting of lively colours upon common truths hath oft a strong working both upon the fancy and our will and affections'.[14] These 'lively colours' served to enhance the appeal of 'common truths' by engaging the heart.[15] As Dever observes, the centrality of the heart was clear in Sibbes' conception of depravity, conversion, motivation, assurance, backsliding, and sanctification.

Just how did Sibbes engage the heart? His most well-known work *The Bruised Reed* – a collection of sermons on Jesus' quotation of Isaiah 42:1-3 – highlights several of his primary strategies. The following section demonstrates how Sibbes so effectively applied the gospel to the hearts of his hearers using examples from this work.

Gospel Mercy for Bruised Reeds

First, *Sibbes articulated the gospel in terms of Trinitarian harmony*. His words emphasized the unified foundation that the Father, Son, and Spirit give to redemption. The Father is pleased with the work of the Son, which the Spirit applies to the heart of the believer. In this 'sweet agreement of all three persons', the Christian finds comfort.[16] By drawing attention to the coordinated effort within the Trinitarian community

---

14 Richard Sibbes, 'The Soul's Conflict with Itself,' in *Works of Richard Sibbes*, ed. Alexander B. Grosart (1862-64; repr., Carlisle, PA: Banner of Truth, 1979), 1:184.

15 Dever points out that Sibbes used the terms will, affections, desires, and heart interchangeably (Dever, *Richard Sibbes*, 143).

16 Richard Sibbes, *The Bruised Reed*, Puritan Paperbacks (1630; repr., Edinburgh: Banner of Truth Trust, 2008), 56-57.

on behalf of the believer, Sibbes invited his audience to look beyond themselves for assurance. Unity within the Godhead provided a sturdier defense against discouragement than 'the fig leaves of morality'.[17]

Second, *Sibbes applied the gospel with practical precision.* He employed the language of Scripture to address the greatest concerns of a troubled conscience. The 'bruised reed' should embrace the work of God in his life, however painful it might be, for, as Sibbes put it, 'It is better to go bruised to heaven than sound to hell.'[18] The 'smoking flax' must remember how God views him, despite his failures and meager faith. Christ considers not just who we are, but who He will make us to be. You may feel like nothing but a smoldering spark, but God's grace can fan that spark into a flame. Such words of encouragement were accompanied by practical instructions in how to engage the means by which Christ preserves His grace in His people. In *The Bruised Reed,* Sibbes specifically encouraged regular communion with other believers, the practice of holy duties, attending regular preaching, and, most importantly, the exercise of grace through spiritual obedience.

Third, as has been demonstrated, *Sibbes illustrated the gospel with powerful pictures that strengthened his points.* He did not merely say, 'See great things in little beginnings.' He mused, 'See a flame in a spark, a tree in a seed.'[19] He not only called weary Christians to look to Christ, but advised, 'When we feel ourselves cold in affection and duty, the best way is to warm ourselves at this fire of his love and mercy.'[20] For believers who

---

17 Sibbes, *ibid.,* 4.

18 Sibbes, *ibid.,* 13.

19 Sibbes, *ibid.,* 124.

20 Sibbes, *ibid.,* 81.

longed to maintain a tender heart, Sibbes encouraged, 'Use the means of grace; be always under the sunshine of the gospel.'[21] Such images conveyed truth by engaging the imagination. As Sibbes explained in another work, 'The way to come to the heart is often to pass through the fancy [imagination].... It was our saviour Christ's manner of teaching to express heavenly things in an earthly manner.'[22]

Fourth, *he applied the gospel with tender, balanced encouragement.* Sibbes counseled pastors to handle young believers with gentleness and to resist the temptation to be overbearing. A tender Savior should not inspire ill-tempered shepherds. That Sibbes managed such a disposition himself seems clear from his reputation among contemporaries and the way he was remembered by his colleagues. Sibbes' diplomatic temperament may have contributed to his willingness to remain in the Church of England, even as some of his protégés began to dissent. In *The Bruised Reed*, Sibbes indirectly cautioned his comrades against being quick to censure other believers or to break fellowship over disputable matters. He valued tact and discretion, remarking, 'Where most holiness is, there is most moderation.'[23]

Finally, and most significantly, *Sibbes' preaching was thoroughly Christ-centered.* In the Son of God, Sibbes proclaimed, 'All perfections of mercy and love meet.'[24] Sibbes spoke often of Christ and tied his expositions to the Son's person and work. By drawing the heart's attention to the mercy of Christ, Sibbes could counter discouragements, calm scruples,

---

21 Sibbes, *The Tender Heart,* 57.

22 *Works of Richard Sibbes*, 1:66.

23 Sibbes, *The Bruised Reed*, 33.

24 Sibbes, *ibid.,* 62.

and conquer the deepest fears of unworthiness. Whatever the spiritual infirmity, the work of Christ supplies the cure. Or, as Sibbes famously put it, 'There is more mercy in Christ than sin in us.'[25] With tender affection and balanced application, illustrated with powerful images grounded in the unity of God, Sibbes preached Christ to the heart.

The Appropriate Remedy

Pastor, do you know how to apply the gospel to your heart? Are you ready to counter the inescapable doubts of your own conscience? Are you prepared to face the difficulties that accompany a lifetime of keeping watch over eternal souls? Reflecting on his own experiences, Lloyd-Jones remarked, 'I pity the preacher who does not know the appropriate remedy to apply to himself in these various phases through which his spiritual life must inevitably pass.'[26]

Pastors must not only seek out the cure for their own spiritual ailments, they also must proclaim the truth gently and tenderly week after week, even as their sermons address weary congregations. Just as pastors can get overwhelmed, so can the people in the pews. Their hearts become troubled and their souls grow tired. They need truth, but they also need encouragement. Sibbes reminds us of the pastor's call to shepherd the heart back to Christ. There are many bruised reeds in your midst. Will you lend them strength or increase their burdens? There are smoldering wicks before you. Will you fan them into life or snuff them out? Pastors do well to bear in mind the tender mercy of our Savior as they endeavor to lead hearts toward His light and easy yoke.

---

25   Sibbes, *ibid.*, 33.

26   Lloyd-Jones, *Preaching and Preachers*, 175.

Richard Baxter (1615–1691)

Pastor, Kidderminster Church (England)

Primary Works

The Reformed Pastor
Christian Directory
The Saint's Everlasting Rest

Mentors

William Perkins, Richard Sibbes

'I preached, as never sure to preach again, and as a dying man to dying men.' (Richard Baxter)

10.

The Pastor's Shepherding
with Richard Baxter

In the last fifty years, pastoral handbooks have often followed a familiar script. A well-known pastor shares his congregation's success story, explaining how they got where they are today. He acknowledges the work of God and quotes the Bible here and there, but the focus tends to be on his cleverness and courage. Strategies and methods overshadow theology. Biblical standards are assumed instead of articulated. Whether intended or not, the basic message is often, 'The end has already justified the means, so go and do as I have done.'

If you are reading this book, there is a good chance you have a distaste for this kind of pragmatism. Yet, such stories are appealing in their own way. In fact, it is tempting to try to fit Richard Baxter's famous work *The Reformed Pastor* into this very mold. Just consider his own description of God's work in the English town of Kidderminster during his ministry:

The congregation was usually full, so that we were fain to build five galleries after my coming. Our private meetings also were full. On the Lord's Days, there was no disorder to be seen in the streets, but you might hear an hundred families singing psalms and repeating sermons.... In a word, when I came first, there was about one family in a street that worshipped God and called on his name; and when I came away, there were some streets where there was not passed one family in the side of the street that did not so, and that did not, by professing serious godliness, give us hope of their sincerity.[1]

Who wouldn't want to grow a church to the point of requiring expansion of the facilities? Who doesn't desire to see their town transformed? Who would not be interested in hearing how Baxter accomplished this? And yet, the man behind this ministry would not have us employ his method without first understanding his convictions. He was not leading his congregation based on the latest trends; he was simply trying to pastor as the Bible commanded. Baxter is a helpful example to today's pastors, not just because his method proved fruitful, but because it was rooted in the biblical call to shepherd the flock.

The Life and Ministry of Richard Baxter

Baxter was born in 1615 in a small village in Shropshire. His formal education was minimal, but he trained himself on a steady diet of what he called 'our old English practical divinity'.[2] His reading of William Perkins and Richard Sibbes and other early Puritans provided a foundation for his future ministry and influenced his eventual conflicts with the Church of England.

---

1   Richard Baxter, *Reliquiae Baxterianae*, ed. Matthew Sylvester (London, 1696), 79.

2   Referenced in Eamon Duffy, foreword to *Richard Sibbes: Puritanism and Calvinism in Late Elizabethan and Early Stuart England*, by Mark Dever (Macon, GA: Mercer University Press, 2000).

In 1641, after a brief stint as an educator and pastoral assistant, he was appointed lecturer in Kidderminster, a village west of Birmingham. His two-decade ministry there spanned a tumultuous time in British history that included the English Civil War and the short-lived Commonwealth. Despite the political unrest around him, Baxter was remarkably fruitful in these years, publishing over forty books and overseeing the transformation of the town previously referenced.

His later years were further influenced by the political climate of his day. The Restoration of the monarchy in 1660 marked the beginning of a brutal period of persecution for Baxter and his Puritan colleagues. After getting married in 1662, he and his wife, Margaret (1636–1681) relocated to London, where he became a chief spokesman for the Nonconformist party and the frequent target of persecution. Despite multiple imprisonments and notoriously poor health, Baxter continued to publish at a productive pace for the remainder of his life. By the time of his death in 1691, he was considered one of the greatest Puritan theologians who ever lived. Among his many well-known works, the most beloved is perhaps *The Reformed Pastor*, which outlined his approach to pastoral ministry.

Originally compiled as an associational sermon for fellow ministers, *The Reformed Pastor* represents Baxter's mature reflections on pastoral ministry as well as a memoir of sorts of his time at Kidderminster. In true Puritan fashion, we shall examine this work by considering the nature, method, and motives for shepherding set forth by Baxter.

The Nature of Shepherding

The nature of pastoral ministry requires the work to begin in the pastor's own heart. Taking Acts 20:28 as his text, Baxter exhorted ministers to take heed of both themselves and the condition of their flocks. As he warned his fellow pastors, 'That which is most in your hearts, is like to be most in their ears.'[3] So, Baxter exhorted his colleagues to keep watch on their lives, lest their conduct ever discredit their message. He believed that true revival would begin with the clergy: 'If God would but reform the ministry and set them on their duties zealously and faithfully, the people would certainly be reformed. All churches either rise or fall as the ministry doth rise or fall (not in riches or worldly grandeur) but in knowledge, zeal, and ability for their work.'[4]

Just as pastors must take heed of themselves, they should also pay careful attention to their flocks. The nature of this call necessitates intimate knowledge, according to Baxter:

> We must labour to be acquainted, not only with the persons, but with the state of all our people, with their inclinations and conversations; what are the sins of which they are most in danger, and what duties they are most apt to neglect, and what temptations they are most liable to; for if we know not their temperament or disease, we are not likely to prove successful physicians.[5]

Along with the general call to know the whole flock, Baxter also counseled ministers to give special attention to groups within the flock, including the unconverted, those with a troubled conscience, the truly converted, families, and the sick and dying. In addition, pastors must be willing to lead the church in administering discipline, a practice Baxter

---

3   Richard Baxter, *The Reformed Pastor* (1656; repr., Carlisle, PA: Banner of Truth Trust, 2007), 61.

4   Baxter, *Reliquiae Baxterianae*, 115.

5   Baxter, *The Reformed Pastor*, 90.

considered to be far too infrequent among English clergymen. Providing step-by-step instructions, he urged his colleagues to discipline the impenitent among them in the interest of both the church's witness and the unruly member's soul. Baxter followed the Calvinist tradition in believing that discipline was a key responsibility of the shepherd.

When preaching, Baxter sought to expound the fundamentals of the faith with clarity and conviction. He did not consider his sermon ready until it was intelligible to all, regardless of the spiritual maturity of his hearers. 'There is no better way to make a good cause prevail, than to make it as plain, and as generally and thoroughly known as we can,' he remarked.[6] Throughout his life, Baxter was burdened by many bodily infirmities; Packer called him a 'veritable museum of disease'.[7] While no doubt making his labors more difficult, his frequent ailments may well have strengthened his ministry by reminding him how short life could be. Thus, he preached, as he so eloquently stated, 'as a dying man to dying men.'[8] In a similar vein, Baxter urged his fellow pastors to conduct themselves in dependence upon God.

The Method of Shepherding

Baxter's method involved a tireless regimen of educating his people in biblical thought and practice. This methodology was influenced by his ecclesiastical context – after the Civil War,

---

6   Baxter, *ibid.*, 116.

7   J. I. Packer, *A Grief Sanctified: Through Sorrow to Eternal Hope* (1997; repr., Wheaton, IL: Crossway, 2002), quoted in Michael Haykin, *The Reformers and Puritans as Spiritual Mentors* (Dundas, Ontario: Joshua Press, 2012), 148.

8   Richard Baxter, *Poetical Fragments* (1681; repr., London: Samuel and Richard Bentley, 1821), 35.

Baxter concluded that his energy was best spent toward the transformation of the soul rather than structural improvements – and somewhat necessitated by his predecessor's negligence (who was known for spending more time in the tavern than the pulpit).[9] So, Baxter taught his people. He taught them publicly, preaching twice per week and hosting a weekly forum to entertain theological questions; and he taught them privately, working with his assistant to catechize annually the eight hundred families in the town. While his preaching ministry focused on educating his people in the fundamentals of doctrine, these private meetings were aimed at assessing a person's spiritual condition and counseling them toward Christ.

Baxter did not invent catechizing, but he can be rightly credited for popularizing the practice in England. In a letter written around the time of *The Reformed Pastor*, he described the process to a friend.[10] After giving notice in the public meeting, his assistant Richard Sargent would give each family a booklet that contained the Apostle's Creed, the Ten Commandments, and the Lord's Prayer along with a twelve-question catechism written by Baxter. He considered it important to provide the catechism to the family, even if it meant paying for it out of pocket, lest the expense become an excuse for not participating. Families would then have six weeks to study the material and (ideally) commit it to

---

9   According to Nuttall, Baxter's predecessor George Dance 'preached but once a quarter' and was considered a frequent drunkard (Geoffrey F. Nuttall, *Richard Baxter* [London: Thomas Nelson, 1965], 25).

10 Cited in Kelly M. Kapic and Randall C. Gleason, *The Devoted Life: An Invitation to the Puritan Classics* (Downers Grove, IL: InterVarsity Press, 2004), 160.

memory. He encouraged his fellow pastors to deal gently with anyone who struggled with memorization, being more concerned about the person's heart than their power of recall. After this time, either Baxter or his assistant would personally catechize the members of the family, typically hosting around fifteen families per week. In these sessions, he would go over the material with each person individually, asking them to not only recite the answers but also explain the meaning of weightier doctrines. As he instructed others to follow this example, Baxter encouraged the minister to be mindful at all times of the person's mental and emotional state – the goal was to affirm and increase knowledge of God, not to embarrass or befuddle. When it became clear that a person did not know an answer, Baxter would have the minister instruct them clearly and carefully, seizing the opportunity to apply truth with precision. In *The Reformed Pastor*, he provided examples of what a minister could say in such moments, including how to apply the gospel to the heart of one who is clearly unconverted. Throughout the whole exercise, he emphasized the necessity of a minister conducting himself in such a way that would 'convince his people of his ability, sincerity, and unfeigned love to them.'[11]

Baxter testified to the effectiveness of this practice: 'I have found by experience that some ignorant persons, who have been so long unprofitable hearers, have got more knowledge and remorse in half an hour's close discourse, than they did from ten years' public preaching.'[12] While continuing to believe in the power of preaching, he made personal conversations a priority, recognizing how significant such interactions could

---

11   Baxter, *The Reformed Pastor*, 232.

12   Baxter, *ibid.*, 196.

be in the hand of God. Though tiresome at times, these conversations were a source of great joy to Baxter: 'Of all the works that I ever attempted, this yielded me most comfort in the practice of it.'[13]

The Motivation for Shepherding

Several motivations provided the fuel for Baxter's fire. Ministers should embrace their work because, as Acts 20 makes clear, they are entrusted with oversight of the flock. As a parish minister, Baxter considered his flock to include the entire town, chastising himself and his colleagues for not laboring toward the salvation of each and every soul. A pastor should not be 'an idol for the people to bow down to' nor 'idle' in his labors, but rather 'the guide of sinners to heaven.'[14] Such great responsibility calls for the prudent use of all possible means, including catechetical efforts aimed at both discipleship and evangelism.

Baxter encouraged pastors to be motivated by the call they had received from the Holy Spirit, confirmed by the church. Because the Spirit of God appointed them to the work, they should labor with confidence that the Spirit would give power to their efforts. Finally, Baxter reminded pastors that their church belonged to God because He redeemed its people through the death of His Son. 'Every time we look upon our congregations,' he exhorted, 'let us believingly remember that they are the purchase of Christ's blood, and therefore should be regarded by us with the deepest interest and the most tender affection.'[15] With these things in mind, pastors should labor

---

13 Baxter, *Reliquiae Baxterianae*, 84.

14 Baxter, *The Reformed Pastor*, 125.

15 Baxter, *ibid.*, 132.

to do all they can to shepherd their flocks, 'searching men's hearts, and setting home the truth to their consciences.'[16]

A Call to Shepherd

A brief survey of Baxter's ministry reveals many differences between his context and our own. The work of God in Kidderminster was certainly unique at the time. However, his posture as a shepherd toward his flock was a faithful application of biblical convictions. Modern ministers might not approach their congregations in exactly the same way as Baxter, but much can be learned from his ministry of shepherding.

Regardless of context, *the pastor's central task is to shepherd his people.* The method and means of accomplishing this goal should be adjusted to the church and the pastor, but the task remains the same. The call to pastor is a call to shepherd, whether in first-century Ephesus or sixteenth-century England.

Regardless of temperament, *pastors must know their people and their needs.* Baxter gave step-by-step instructions for how to attain such knowledge; his method must be contextualized, but no one should let their personality excuse them from this important aspect of ministry. Pastors do not merely preach sermons or teach doctrine; they lead people to the truth. To do so effectively, they must know their people as well as they know the truth.

Finally, regardless of perceived needs, *pastors must remember that what will benefit their people most is more of God.* Baxter labored to help people come to a better understanding of the person and work of God. He preached and counseled and catechized to that end. Today's pastors would do well to follow in his footsteps.

---

16   Baxter, *ibid.*, 46.

John Eliot (1604–1690)

Pastor, Roxbury Church, Massachusetts Bay Colony
Missionary to the Massachusett Indians

Primary Works

Bay Psalm Book
The Christian Commonwealth
The Eliot Bible
Indian Grammar Begun

Mentor

Thomas Hooker (1586–1647)

*'Christ Jesus taketh possession of the heathen, and utmost ends
of the earth; and this is one description of our Country. And
now Jesus Christ calleth us to come to him. Some of us have
submitted unto Christ, and he hath mercifully accepted us, and
so he will accept you if you will come in unto him.'* (John Eliot)

11.

The Pastor's Evangelism
with John Eliot

A dusty and worn fedora. A loaded revolver. A coiled bullwhip. A perennial five o'clock shadow. These were not the usual marks of a tenured professor in the 1930s; however, the unique and provocative were common for Dr. Henry Walton Jones, Jr. (or Indiana, as he is better known). Jones was an archaeology professor, but also a daring adventurer. On the one hand he fits the mold of the researcher and teacher, while on the other he uncharacteristically explored remote and exotic settings to combat would-be thieves and thwart global domination. He fulfilled both roles to achieve aligned objectives – to secure and protect rare artifacts so that the world could enjoy them.

Not unlike the fictional Indiana Jones, history primarily remembers John Eliot (1604–1690) for his most daring exploit – an unconventional mission to the Native Americans of New England. Eliot's commitment to his objective – establishing churches that honored the Lord – shaped his approach to both his beloved congregation at Roxbury and the Massachusetts Indians.

Eliot's Dual Vocation as Pastor and Missionary

John Eliot was born in Widford in Hertfordshire in August 1604. After growing up in Nazing in Essex, he was educated at Jesus College, Cambridge, and eventually taught at Little Baddow in Essex. Thomas Hooker (1586–1647) served as the headmaster of the school, and it was under his mentorship and preaching that Eliot was converted.

After Hooker left England in 1630 – under pressure as a nonconformist – Eliot also departed, setting out for New England. He arrived in Massachusetts on November 3, 1631, motivated by the desire to 'enjoy the holy worship of God, not according to the fantasies of man, but according to the Word of God.'[1] Shortly after arriving in the Bay Colony, Eliot accepted a temporary position as pastor of the Boston church. When John Wilson, the permanent pastor, returned from England in the summer of 1632, the church requested that Eliot remain as teaching elder. He declined this post, as he intended to serve among his friends from Nazing, who were now members of the church in Roxbury.

Thomas Weld (c.1595–1661) served as the minister of the Roxbury congregation where Eliot was ordained as teaching elder in November 1632. As Richard Cogley notes, Eliot may have been the first minister in the Bay Colony who was not 'previously ordained by an Anglican bishop.'[2]

The Pastor and His People

Eliot served the Roxbury church as teaching elder, or pastor, from 1632 to 1688, over a half-century of faithful service with

1   John Eliot, quoted in Cotton Mather, *Magnalia Christi Americana* (London, 1698), 1:335-36.

2   Richard Cogley, *John Eliot's Mission to the Indians Before King Philip's War* (Cambridge, MA: Harvard, 1999), 46.

one congregation.[3] A pastoral tenure this long is rare under any circumstances, particularly since over thirty-five of those years were also spent in pioneering work among the Indians. A pastor may often speak of 'his people'. The phrase can simply express sentiment or it may issue from deep-seated conviction. For Congregationalist pastors like Eliot, the notion of a 'fixed', or 'devoted', ministry to a specific congregation (people) was core ideology. This idea was an extension of Calvin's Genevan framework intent on combatting the Roman Catholic practice of ministerial non-residency.[4] Eliot and the Roxbury congregation had been 'wed', and he took the duty to lead these people in this town with great solemnity.

Eliot Shepherded and Served His People

The first-order benefit of pastors genuinely being among their people was that all were known to the shepherd. Knowledge, in Eliot's case, was not devoid of care and deep concern. Ola Winslow notes that the church membership record penned by Eliot around 1646 offers more than simple names and notations: 'Something of the spirit of his entire ministry is in these brief entries. His people were his care, and he knew them. His standards of Christian character were inflexible, but his approach to the erring ones was unfailingly kind.'[5]

Accompanying his strong-minded manner was a patient and kind way that was noticeable not only to his congregation

---

3   Joel Beeke and Randall J. Pederson, *Meet the Puritans* (Grand Rapids: Reformation Heritage, 2007), 235.

4   See Travis Myers, '"Get as Near to God as You Can": The Congregationalist Piety and Cross-Cultural Ministry of John Eliot (1604-1690)' (PhD diss., Boston University, 2015), 60.

5   Ola Winslow, *John Eliot: Apostle to the Indians* (Boston: Houghton Mifflin, 1968), 35.

but also to his contemporaries. Cotton Mather (1663–1728) reflected on Eliot's balanced and humble presence:

> When he heard any ministers complain that such and such in their flocks were too difficult for them, the strain of his answer still was, 'Brother, compass them!' and 'Brother, learn the meaning of those three little words, bear, forbear, fa-give.' Yea, his inclinations for peace, indeed, sometimes almost made him to sacrifice right itself. When there was laid before an assembly of ministers a bundle of papers, which contained certain matters of difference and contention between some people which our Eliot thought should rather unite, with an amnesty upon all their former quarrels, he (with some imitation of what Constantine did upon the like occasion) hastily threw the papers into the fire before them all, and, with a zeal for peace as hot as that fire, said immediately, 'Brethren, wonder not at what I have done: I did it on my knees this morning before I came among you.' Such an excess (if it were one) flowed from his charitable inclinations to be found among those peace-makers which, by following the example of that Man who is our peace, come to be called, 'the children of God.'[6]

This compelling portrait also underscores Eliot's place among this 'assembly of ministers'. He not only served the people through teaching and shepherding, but he also served the needs of the town and the colonies.

Eliot Embraced and Attended to His People

It was common for noted ministers to contribute to the broader concerns of the Bay area, and Eliot was no exception. In 1636 and 1637 alone, he wrote the justification for Roger Williams'

---

6   Mather, *Magnalia Christi Americana*, 1:542.

(1629–1676) banishment and he served in an official capacity during the trial of Anne Hutchinson (1591–1643) over the issue of antinomianism. While these concerns had their impact across the fledgling colonies, Eliot also labored toward the local establishment of the Roxbury grammar school in 1645. The Roxbury Latin School, as it is now named, was established by Eliot and other heads of households.[7] It remains in operation today as a school for boys, and it is America's oldest free and independent school in continuous existence. It was, as Mather noted, 'his perpetual resolution and activity to support a good school in the town that belonged unto him,' that inspired its founding.[8]

He openly, and fervently, encouraged other ministers to establish schools in their towns, in a similar fashion. The priority of accessible education also figured prominently in the missionary method of Eliot. His commitment to education, in every necessary sphere, prompted him to provide resources to equip the New English colonials to learn the Algonquin language, if they chose. To this end, he published *The Indian Grammar Begun* in 1666.[9]

Roxbury, which was south of Boston, occupied the edges of the metropolitan area and began to touch the adjoining wilderness. George Winship observed that this unique geography provided both fewer colonial inhabitants, which freed Eliot's time, and proximity to the native population.[10]

---

7   Winslow, *John Eliot*, 37.

8   Mather, *Magnalia Christi Americana*, 1:551.

9   John Eliot, *The Indian Grammar Begun* (1666; repr., Bedford, MA: Applewood Books, 2001).

10 George Winship, *Introduction to the New England Company of 1649 and John Eliot* (New York: Burt Franklin, 1967), viii.

Eliot's ministry convictions and commitments, along with this unique locale, set the stage for his missionary service.

The Missionary and his Friends

Although these factors did set the stage, it was not free from obstacles. Because of the Congregationalist commitment to local church autonomy, formal missionary service, as that which is commissioned and supported by a local church, was an alien concept. Although Eliot held to congregational residency, as explicitly indicated in his writings to Richard Baxter, Travis Myers has pointed out, 'He held this typically Congregationalist conviction in tension with a grander vision for a global order of church councils that would unify all Reformed congregations, either Congregational or Presbyterian.'[11]

Furthermore, the prospects of cross-cultural ministry undertaken by a Congregationalist pastor faced an inherent challenge. There were no Indian converts to populate native churches. Congregationalist churches were, by definition, established with dedicated ('fixed') pastors. These churches were led and populated by New English colonials. This dynamic added a second layer of complexity. There were no churches to which the natives might belong, precisely because there were no Indian converts.

To make matters even more complicated, the formal statement on colonial ecclesiology, *The Cambridge Platform* (1648), did not provide support for official missionary work. Creativity in approach and method was required; the device with which Eliot sought to overcome the non-inclusion of natives into colonial churches was the 'praying town'.

---

11 Myers, 'Get as Near to God as You Can,' 61.

Eliot's Work to Form Praying Towns

The genesis of Eliot's formal mission to the Massachusett tribes was, by his recollection, a sermon preached in 1646 at Nonantum.[12] By 1674, Eliot had founded fourteen praying towns, with a total population nearing 4,000 inhabitants.[13] Beeke and Pederson describe the sequence and structure of forming these native communities:

> In each town, the natives made a solemn covenant to give themselves and their children 'to God to be his people' as the basis of the new civil government. Eliot organized the new government following Jethro's advice to Moses in Exodus 18; he appointed rulers over hundreds, fifties, and tens in each town to keep law and order. These towns were almost entirely self-governing, though major issues could be referred to Massachusetts General Court.[14]

The objective was to birth local congregations in each town. Eliot founded Natick in 1651, and he formed a Congregationalist church there in 1660. While there were various characteristics of these settlements, there were also familiar elements in Eliot's 'building' approach.

Order for the Sake of Faith

Eliot's emphasis on civility and order, as it pertained to the Indians, was intent on establishing a governmental structure that would optimally support ecclesiastical stability. It is necessary to understand that Eliot's use of the term

---

12   Thomas Shepard, *The Clear Sunshine of the Gospel Breaking Forth upon the Indians in New-England* (London, 1648), 25-26.

13   Beeke and Pederson, *Meet the Puritans*, 236.

14   Beeke and Pederson, *ibid.*, 451.

'civility', and its related cognates 'civilized' and 'civil', was theologically-grounded. The rooting commitments were to 'a commonwealth, covenanted township, a civil government enforcing laws intended to prepare individuals for "gospel" conversion, and the idea of a national covenant whereby God's blessing or curse is corporately instigated and experienced by all citizens.'[15] As Eliot wrote to Thomas Thorowgood in 1660, he labored among the natives so that they might be a 'choice people unto the Lord'.[16] In Eliot's estimation, order was necessary to a life of faith.

Translation for Education and Conversion

Conversion was admittedly the work of God; however, it was a shared conviction in the areas of education and conversion which would necessitate translation of the Bible and supplemental resources. To get to this point required painstaking language acquisition, though Eliot proved well-suited for the task. In 1644, he began language study, in preparation to teach the Massachusett Algonquin tribes.

Translation and writing were already demonstrated capacities for Eliot, as his facility in Hebrew had enabled his contribution to the translation team for the *Bay Psalm Book* (1640), which proved to be the first book printed in British North America. From 1654, with the publication of the first edition of the *Primer and Catechism*, to the printing of his translation of Thomas Shepard's *The Sincere Convert* in

---

15   Myers, 'Get as Near to God as You Can,' 122-23.

16   John Eliot, 'John Eliot to Thomas Thorowgood,' in *The Eliot Tracts: With Letters from John Eliot to Thomas Thorowgood and Richard Baxter*, ed. Michael Clark (Santa Barbara, CA: Praeger, 2003), 426.

1689, Eliot produced twelve total works in the Massachusetts dialect.[17]

Eliot began his translation of the New Testament into the Massachusett dialect in 1653, and published it in 1661, with Old Testament added in 1663. *The Eliot Bible*, as it came to be known, was the first complete Bible printed in America. The production of the completed translation was emblematic of Eliot's guiding conviction that the Bible was to be central in conversion.

The value of instruction, even toward voluntary inclusion through 'conversion', was bolstered by Eliot's translation of specific English Puritan works. A prominent example is the 'Indian library', which consisted of three English titles, translated into Algonquin by Eliot. These volumes were intended to provide a primer for natives that sought to walk by faith in Christ. Richard Baxter's *A Call to the Unconverted* is perhaps most well-known. First published in the native translation in the same timeframe (the 1660s) as Lewis Bayly's *The Practice of Piety*, the second volume in the 'library', Baxter's work served as an apologetic companion volume to Thomas Shephard's *The Sincere Convert*. Shephard's work offered a means to diagnose the sincerity of one's confession of faith.

In educating the native populations, Eliot depended on resources like 'the library'. A critical arena for indigenous instruction and evangelism were the schools Eliot set up in each town. He utilized these schools to both educate and deploy native teachers. As Winslow notes, he trained 'always more than were immediately needed, so that he might have a

---

17 For a full list of all resources, dates of each printing, and which volumes are still extant, see Cogley, 'Appendix 5,' in *John Eliot's Mission to the Indians*, 260.

teacher ready for the next town he founded.'[18] Contextualizing the Bible and related materials through translation, while also training Indian teachers, enabled the native population to develop and lead the praying town.

Indigenous Movement for Native Churches

Understanding this approach to cross-cultural mission, in terms that Eliot would likely affirm, necessitates an appreciation for the Congregationalist commitment to each convert. Whether New English or Native American, each man, woman, and child must belong to a local congregation through membership. This ecclesial conviction was owing to a more comprehensive theological view of the church and civic relationship. As Myers notes,

> In the Congregationalist ideal, Native American converts were to be organized into local congregations that were in connection with other Native and New English congregations. These congregations were each representative of larger local communities, i.e. towns, which shared in common a 'national covenant' with God and one another.[19]

The implication of what Eliot sought to do here is instructive. He moved to establish native towns, which would then form Indian congregations. In tandem, he trained native teachers to carry this work forward. The self-sustainability of this indigenous movement would far exceed 'a mere few individual converts [who] from time to time submit themselves to majority New English congregations and communities.'[20] It

---

18 Winslow, *John Eliot*, 37.

19 Myers, 'Get as Near to God as You Can,' 163.

20 Myers, *ibid.*, 164.

appeared as if the praying town experiment would be a success until a long-brewing battle erupted.

King Philip's War and the End of the Towns

King Philip's War began in June 1675 and lasted until August 1676. The conflict between native tribes on one side and colonists with native allies led to the direct end of ten praying towns and the subsequent unraveling of the remaining four. The Praying Indians, caught between the colonials and native combatants, were decimated by war, starvation, and disease. It was the bloodiest war, per population, in United States history.[21]

It is of note that King Philip's given name was Metacom or Metacomet. He was an intertribal leader of Native Americans in New England. Before the war that would bear his chosen name, he appears to have been a hoped-for convert, in Eliot's estimation. In his *Indian Dialogues*, Eliot portrays interactions that blend historical and instructive elements, as to how conversations with natives have occurred or might unfold in the future. A key figure in the conversations is an intertribal leader named Philip Keitasscot. The character, based on the well-known leader Metacom, was eventually converted, in the pages of *Dialogues*.

Eliot could have included this portrayal for several politically strategic reasons (e.g., to calm colonials' fear of his power, demonstrating he would be under colonial authority). However, more directly, the character of Philip may serve to point to the aspiration of John Eliot, as he sought the conversion

---

21   Robert Cray, "'Weltering in their Own Blood": Puritan Casualties in King Philip's War,' *Historical Journal of Massachusetts* 37, no. 2, Fall 2009: 107.

of this native leader, ever hopeful for tribes to follow him as he followed Christ.

Implications for Pastoral and Cross-Cultural Ministry

Examining the ministry of John Eliot, an earnest pastor who toiled in cross-cultural ministry, can provide insight into our own ministry roles. Here are several implications from his life and ministry, as we develop pastoral practices that are allied with mission advance.

First, *we may theologically and operationally align how we serve the church and field.* Church-planting, teaching, and educational support, for example, could assist to create symmetry between our convictions and our activities, both foreign and domestic.

Second, *we may appropriately contextualize how we serve the church and field.* Notions of colonialism and patriarchy are common accusations against New England Puritans – and, in many cases, such complaints are warranted. However, Eliot's example portrays a man who labored among the native peoples to provide them with the opportunity to read the Bible and other resources in their own language. He established schools and trained native teachers to teach and be deployed to teach among other praying towns, and he protected them from dispossession.

Third, *we may desire conversion and sanctification to occur through the local church.* Eliot sought to see an indigenous movement, rather than periodic converts to New English congregations. To experience conversion and conformity to Christ's image, Eliot held that local congregations provided the means for this to take place.

Fourth, *we may prioritize indigenous church planting in multi-faceted cross-cultural ministry.* The 'praying town' approach sought to provide a means of gospel proclamation, and church founding, to the end that missions movements would privilege church planting while contributing to many other worthwhile pursuits.

Pastor. Missionary. Friend.

John Eliot died on May 20, 1690. Upon his passing, he was still viewed by his congregation as an earnest pastor, 'Ordained over the First Church,' even while he was an 'Apostle to the Indians', as the inscription on his tomb in Roxbury reads. Others remembered him primarily for his missionary role, as memorialized on a meager stone just a few miles away from the first. The inscription here reads:

> In reverent Memory of
> John Eliot
> Born in England 1604
> Died in Roxbury 1690
> Lover of God, Lover of Men
> Seeker of the Christian Commonwealth
> Who on this spot preached
> to his friends the Indians
> in their own tongue
> the mercies and the laws of
> The Eternal
> Pastor. Missionary. Friend.

John Eliot performed each of these roles, for the sake of the gospel, among his people, the church, and his friends – the Indians.

John Cotton (1584–1652)

Teacher, First Church of Boston

Primary Works

The Way of the Churches of Christ in New England
The Keys of the Kingdom of Heaven
The New-England Primer

Mentor

Richard Sibbes

'Those who have found the presence and power of the spirit of Christ breathing in their ministers, either to their conversion, or edification, will be slow to change such a ministry of faith, and holiness, for the liberty of church order.' (John Cotton)

John Winthrop (1588–1649)
Governor, Massachusetts Bay Colony

Primary Works
A Model of Christian Charity
A History of New England

Mentors
Ezekiel Culverwell and John Cotton

12.

The Pastor's Leadership
with John Cotton and John Winthrop

Dodge City, Kansas. A place that recalls frontier legends, rowdy saloons, deadly gunfights, and the names of two men who doggedly tamed the upstart city – Wyatt Earp and Bat Masterson. The strategically-situated location had teetered on a self-destructive fulcrum, seeming to both boom and decay at the same time. Yet, the steely peacekeeping and gritty justice of lawmen Earp and Masterson finally set the town on solid ground, establishing a possible future. Men like that, who bring direction and order in unsteady times, lead with such influence, that their legacies become inseparable from the people and places they served.

In the pioneering years of New England's infancy, John Cotton and John Winthrop are among those legendary names, serving as order-establishing guides to the men, women, and children who would come to call the American Colonies 'home'. These two men shared a common era, while providing diverse examples of Christ-exalting leadership, displayed in overlapping but distinct spheres of colonial life. While Cotton is primarily remembered for his pastoral ministry, Winthrop is known for his vision and effort on behalf of society at-large.

Cotton was a 'pastor among pastors', and Winthrop – the credited founder of New England – a looming public figure, shaped by 'religious, political, and economic forces in England', which fed his appetite to 'impose his will on history'.[1] With daunting obstacles before them, in the contexts of fledgling settlements and recently established churches, these men sought to organize, lead, and further develop a defined culture, trusting in the providential care of God.

A Leader among Leaders: Winthrop and the Vision for Sound Leadership

In late March of 1630, John Winthrop had finally assembled a fleet, preparing to make the journey to the New World. In this process, he had determined to sell Groton Manor, which had been both his home and career station, opting to discontinue his vocation as landlord for the opportunity to serve as governor for the Massachusetts Bay Colony. As they prepared to embark, Winthrop had arranged for John Cotton to address the company, likely at the Church of the Holy Rood, located in the Southampton port.[2]

Cotton preached to the assembly, which included some from his own congregation in Lincolnshire. The sermon was entitled 'God's Promise to His Plantation'. Winthrop followed Cotton's message with his own sermon, which would later be

1   Francis Bremer, *John Winthrop: Biography as History* (New York: Continuum, 2009), 1-2.

2   Bremer notes that Southampton historians substantiate the reality of Cotton presiding over the service in approximately that timeframe and location (Francis Bremer, *John Winthrop: America's Forgotten Founding Father* [Oxford: University Press, 2003], 173-74, 431).

called 'The Model of Christian Charity'. The task for Winthrop, not only in the poignant moment of an inspirational address, but in the far more demanding leadership responsibility of hammering out the call of this homily, was to see God forge a rugged brand of unity and charity among a disparate group of Puritan Pilgrims.

Winthrop not only embraced the duty to help the group envision their responsibility, but he masterfully handled the moment. Bremer remarks, 'No other work of colonial literature has been as frequently anthologized.'[3] He concluded the sermon with these galvanizing words:

> We must be knit together in this work as one man, we must entertain each other in brotherly affection, we must be willing to abridge ourselves of our superfluities for the supply of others' necessities, we must delight in each other, mourn together, labor and suffer together, always having before our eyes our Commission and Community in the work.[4]

Borrowing language from the pages of the New Testament at most every turn, Winthrop offered the voyagers a depiction of their preferred future, rooting every image in the sure past. He had been master of the manor, but now his charge was to be captain of a perilous voyage, seeing it through to the Colony. He would then lead these same people in establishing life in a foreign land, exhibiting the hearty dexterity required of someone thrust into a range of leadership situations and differing environments.

---

3 Bremer, *John Winthrop*, 174.

4 The full sermon manuscript is rendered in *The Journal of John Winthrop: 1630-1649*, abridged ed., ed. Richard Dunn and Laetitia Yeandle (Cambridge, MA: Belknap Press, 1996), 1-11.

Winthrop understood that he was not a pastor, as Cotton knew that he was not a civil servant. However, neither of these leaders abdicated the call to theological propriety in thinking and acting, understanding this approach as a means by which those in Christ love their neighbor. This thinking was to influence Winthrop's leadership approach and the values that such guidance was intended to reinforce. Among these values was the notion that the leadership was provided to encourage both the individual *and* the community to act for the good of all. This was the 'Commission and Community in the work' of establishing the commonwealth. Winthrop would borrow from the Sermon on the Mount to remind the travelers what was at stake as they established 'a City upon a Hill' in the New World (Matt. 5:14-16).

A Pastor among Pastors: Cotton and the Craft of Pastoral Leadership

Though any number of Puritan figures could offer a pattern for shepherd leadership, John Cotton inhabits rare space. Arriving in the Bay Colony in September 1633, he soon took the post of Teacher at the First Church of Boston. In New England, he proved to be both faithful in local church ministry and vastly influential among ministry students, pastors, and even those in civil government. Influence on this scale owes largely to a keen awareness of, what Cotton called, the 'instrumentality' of pastoral ministry, as employed by God. The forged tools of preaching, writing, and his broader pastoral life were the marrow of Cotton's leadership practice.[5]

As all who serve the church come to understand, gospel ministers are challenged, tested, and pressured leaders. Cotton

5   Sargent Bush, ed., *The Correspondence of John Cotton* (Chapel Hill: University of North Carolina Press, 2001), 1-2.

was certainly no exception. His role, and related actions, in a series of memorable cases indicate that he maintained commitments to: (1) contend for gospel truth; (2) display pointed conviction; and (3) share leadership responsibility with others. Exploring these example cases should provide insight for pastors who face challenges, conflicts, and even congregational crises today.

Pastors Contend for Truth: The Antinomian Controversy and Anne Hutchinson

In the late 1630s, Cotton preached a sermon series entitled *A Treatise of the Covenant of Grace*. Focusing on matters of divine grace and sovereignty, he explained how these doctrines inform perspectives on human responsibility, addressing the relationship between justification and sanctification.[6] With Cotton mining this theological bedrock, members of the First Church of Boston responded exuberantly, celebrating the reality of the merciful work of the Holy Spirit to bring conversion.

Among them was Anne Hutchinson, having followed Cotton to the Bay Colony in 1634. While her husband William was tasked with extensive political responsibility, as Deputy from Boston to the Massachusetts General Court, Anne took up the mantle of spiritual advisor to the local women, holding

---

6   Paul Schaefer notes that Cotton was dedicated to dealing with dicey theological issues as a means of practical need for the congregations and the colonies: 'The correlation between grace and works, the abilities and inabilities of human agents, the Spirit's work through means given to the institutional church and apart from such means, and salvation as a divine apprehension and/or process all received careful attention.' Paul Schaefer, *The Spiritual Brotherhood: Cambridge Puritans and the Nature of Christian Piety* (Grand Rapids: Reformation Heritage, 2011), 267-68.

weekly meetings to discuss the sermons from the previous Lord's Day. Hosting as many as sixty participants, Hutchinson reviewed Cotton's message, while also raising questions as to the quality of other preachers, eventually accusing them of preaching 'works' rather than 'grace'. She had pushed past the ostensibly more balanced stance of her pastor, stepping into territory fraught with peril and confusion, which eventually gave way to antinomianism and brought her impressionable followers out of bounds alongside her.

As an earnest pastor, Cotton ultimately responded to these developments with compassion and humility. Humbly compassionate contention may seem an errant phrase, but the ability to actively reconcile these chief marks of a Christ-emulating shepherd-servant is a necessary practice for pastoral leaders. That truth is of utmost concern, if any dark fault in our teaching and leading must see the light of confession and repentance.

Cotton would ultimately have to come to terms with his own unwitting laxity in watchfulness and precision, as well as his need to maintain fidelity and unity, among the elders in Boston.[7] At the point of Hutchinson's trial, Cotton acknowledged, 'It may be it was my sleepiness and want of watchful care' that allowed for her views to bloom, yet he also recognized the need for correction:

> I must needs say that I have often feared the height of your spirit and being puffed up with your own parts, and therefore it is just with God thus to abase you and to leave you to these desperate

---

7   Schaefer, *The Spiritual Brotherhood*, 267-68.

falls for the Lord looks upon all the children of pride and delights to abase them and bring them low.[8]

Cotton was not directly responsible for Hutchinson's wayward views, but his reflections demonstrate the need for precision and clarity to serve as sentries of our preaching and shepherding.

After extensive elder and magistrate deliberation, Hutchinson and her family were expelled from the community on March 22, 1638. A decade later, Cotton would write *The Way of Congregational Churches Cleared* (1648), offering not simply a declaration of congregationalist polity, but a sympathetic picture of the dedicated work that Hutchinson had performed among women in the colony, by which 'she found loving and dear respect both from our Church-Elders and Brethren, and so from myself also amongst the rest.' Cotton goes on to speak of Hutchinson and her family as 'dear unto me' and of Anne specifically as 'my dear friend, till she turned aside.'[9]

The convergence of theological, ecclesial, and political forces, mingled with the personal recognition of Hutchinson's turn from cherished friend to errant foe, ultimately pushed Cotton to recognize his contribution to the controversy – he had failed to be precise in his teaching or vigilant in his shepherding.[10] In so doing, he affirmed the close relationship between the ecclesial and civil realms, in order that the blossoming colony could rightly flourish.

---

8   'A Report of the Trial of Mrs. Ann Hutchinson before the Church in Boston, March 1638,' in *The Antinomian Controversy, 1636-1638: A Documentary History*, ed. David Hall (Middletown, CT: Wesleyan University Press, 1968), 372.

9   John Cotton, 'Way of Congregational Churches Cleared,' in *The Antinomian Controversy, 1636-1638: A Documentary History*, ed. David Hall, 2nd ed. (Durham, NC: Duke University Press, 1990), 413.

10   Schaefer, *The Spiritual Brotherhood*, 300.

Pastors Display Conviction: The Disputes with Roger Williams

Roger Williams (c.1603–1683) did not share Cotton's view of the relationship between civil government and the church. While Cotton held hope that the colony would be shaped civically by the foundational essentials of a shared theology and ecclesiology, in the mold of a Bible Commonwealth, Williams vehemently maintained the need for separation of church and state through his ministry at the Salem Church.[11] Not unlike Hutchinson, Williams would experience the providential outworking of more precise Puritan thought, which would ultimately not allow for Separatist expression.

Ultimately, Williams was banished from Massachusetts on October 9, 1635. Cotton vehemently maintained that he was not consulted before the magistrates moved forward with the exile, but Williams held tightly to the suspicion that Cotton was directly responsible for his punishment. Cotton's letter to Williams, in early 1636, demonstrates a vital dual commitment, as he desired to see reconciliation and repentance – the impulse to act in earnest conviction by caring for both the work of God *and* the worth of people. In the message, Cotton made clear that the expulsion 'was neither done by my counsel nor consent, although I dare not deny the sentence passed to be righteous in the eyes of God.'[12] He also exhorted Williams

---

11   Williams briefly served in Plymouth, before returning to Salem in 1633, because he was dissatisfied with the insufficiency of Separatist commitment among the Pilgrims (Francis Bremer, *The Puritan Experiment: New England Society from Bradford to Edwards*, rev. ed. [Lebanon, NH: University of New England Press, 1995], 62-64).

12   'A Letter of Mr. John Cotton, Teacher of the Church of Boston, in New-England, to Mr. Williams as Preacher There,' in *The Correspondence of Roger Williams, 1629-53*, vol. 1, ed. Glenn

not to 'let any prejudice against my person (I beseech you) forestall either your affection or judgment' as he pointed out the 'sandiness' of the 'grounds' for teaching on separation.

Cotton's stated aim was not 'to add affliction to your affliction, but (if it were the holy will of God) to move you to a more serious sight of your sin.'[13] Cotton's example supports the corrective that conviction is not inherently opposed to caring. In fact, conviction can be the very proof of care. Biblical conviction, under the lordship and leadership of Christ, should foster humility shown in loving courage.[14]

Pastors Share Leadership: The Cambridge Synod and Platform

During this time, as Separatism was categorized as beyond the bounds, the counterpart need for an approved church polity and governance became evident. In 1646, with Presbyterian and sectarian Puritan groups exerting heightened influence on thought and practice in the colonies, Cotton was enlisted to serve on a committee as part of the Synod at Cambridge. Working alongside Richard Mather (1596–1669) and Ralph Partridge (1579–1658), Cotton outlined an acceptable model of church government.

The result of his influence, through written and deliberative communication, was to place an indelible mark on the embraced Congregationalism in New England. Even though

---

LaFantasie (Hanover, NH: University Press of New England, 1988), 33-34.

13 'A Letter of Mr. John Cotton to Mr. Williams,' 33-34.

14 The focus of their correspondence would ultimately shift to religious tolerance. Even here, as the intensity of the debate heightened, Cotton sought to call his opponent to repentance. These debates took place from 1644 to 1652, and the *Bloody Tenent* writings provide a reliable outline of the matters in dispute.

Cotton's writings formed much of the foundation on which the 'New England Way' was to be built, his approach to this process demonstrates a desire to share leadership. *The Cambridge Platform*, adopted in 1648, established these doctrinal norms and expectations for Congregationalist churches in New England. It was also decisively informed by Cotton's prior writings, as well as those penned by Richard Mather.[15]

The ability to work in concert with these leaders is informative, as Cotton had debated with some of them during the Antinomian Controversy involving Hutchinson. Numbered among those men was Mather, who had vocally criticized Cotton's own views and failure to discipline Hutchinson. Cotton's teachable spirit and deference to other leaders appears striking. He would need to coordinate efforts with a man who had once rebuked and publicly challenged his orthodoxy. However, in the spirit of Winthrop's own words, which rest on scriptural notions of faith, Cotton and Mather sought to 'labor together', precisely because they recognized the work that they performed on behalf of the church was more significant than themselves.

Cotton and Winthrop: Serving as Brothers, Leading as Friends

The individual emphases and strokes of each respective leadership approach are only enhanced by the unique friendship that these two men shared. Today, the word 'friendship' is sometimes used to describe what is nothing more than vague acquaintance, the

---

15 Cotton's key works, in addressing congregational polity, are: *The Way of the Churches of Christ in New England* (1641); and *The Keys of the Kingdom of Heaven, and the Power Thereof* (1644). Richard Mather's noted works, as to church governance, are *An Apology of the Churches in New-England*, and *Church-Government and Church-Covenant*, which were both published in 1643.

social media landscape obscuring its meaning. Carelessly, we use the term to gain interest and indicate supposed relational proximity. However, Cotton and Winthrop shared a genuine friendship, which was shaped by the uncommon circumstances in which they led. When Winthrop became gravely ill, in 1648, Cotton called the church to pray for their leader:

> Upon this occasion, we are now to attend to this duty for a governor, who has been to us as a friend in his counsel for all things, and help for our bodies by physic, for our estates by law, and of whom there was no fear of becoming an enemy, like the friends of David; a governor who has been unto us as a brother, not usurping authority over the church, often speaking his advice, and often contradicted, even by young men, and some of low degree, yet not replying, but offering satisfaction also when any supposed offenses have arisen; a governor who has been unto us as a mother, parent-like distributing his goods to brothers and neighbors at this first coming, and gently bearing our infirmities without taking notice of them.[16]

Cotton was present with his 'friend' and 'brother' in his final days and hours, having shared in the labor of trusting God to establish a commonwealth – labor that warranted defense of the truth, convictional action, and a dependent community of leaders. Such were the marks of their friendship, which served to sustain them as they led in perilous times. In this way, Winthrop and Cotton provide a helpful example to pastors today, both in their gritty resolve and in their willingness to lean on one another.

---

16   This statement was an application of his treatment of Psalms 13 and 14. For the full notation, see Cotton Mather, *Magnalia Christi Americana, Books I and II*, ed. Kenneth Murdock (Cambridge, MA: Belknap Press, 1977), 227-28.

Jonathan Edwards (1703–1758)

Pastor, Northampton, Stockbridge; President, College of New Jersey

Primary Works

A Treatise Concerning Religious Affections
The Life of David Brainerd
Freedom of the Will

Mentor

Solomon Stoddard (1643–1729)

'Christians need constant reminders of how amazingly glorious our great God really is and what his glory means for our lives.'
(Jonathan Edwards)

13.

The Pastor's Failures
with Jonathan Edwards

Every pastor will fail. Some will endure great consequences that undermine a lifetime of ministry. Others will discover that doctrinal errors have led them toward unbiblical practices. The Scriptures are full of fallen saints. The history of the church has followed course. Sin lurks in every heart (Rom. 3:9-18), Satan prowls at every turn (1 Pet. 5:8), and each generation faces new challenges (e.g., Judg. 2:11-15); some failures are most clear to those who follow in their footsteps (1 Cor. 10:6).

Pastors do well to sit quietly under such truths. This should inform our response to the latest scandal as well as our appraisal of historical heroes. In this book, we have highlighted some of the many lessons that today's pastors can learn from the Puritans. As the heralds of a movement that stretched across the Atlantic and spanned over two centuries, Puritan pastors left behind many examples of faithfulness, godliness, and courageous conviction. Yet, their collective legacy is not without stains. Many of the men mentioned in this work owned slaves. Some defended the institution passionately. Others held views on women or certain classes of people that fall short of a biblical vision of human dignity. Their churches were far from flawless and some of their theological emphases were skewed, owing more to the zeitgeist of their day than the precision of their exegesis. So, why should we continue to listen to such flawed leaders? Do their blind spots discredit their vision for the church and the work of a pastor?

This chapter will aim to answer these questions by examining the failures of one of the Puritan movement's most-celebrated figures. Jonathan Edwards is generally recognized as the greatest theologian in American history. His ministry in western Massachusetts helped spark the Great Awakening and his writings continue to inspire scores of articles, dissertations, and monographs each year. He has been a gift to the church and yet his own congregation forced him from his post. He was steeped in a social hierarchy that both contributed to his prominence and prejudiced his view of others, including the slaves he and his wife owned. His story is a reminder to us all that even the brightest of minds have dark corners, capable of moral inconsistencies. Even faithful pastors may find themselves without a job. Edwards is in many ways a culmination of the Puritan movement; in other ways, he represents some of its regrettable consequences. Acknowledging his historical context is necessary; yet allowing that context to serve as a cover for his flaws would be wrong. With hopes of providing a balanced picture, this chapter considers the life, ministry, and failures of the great Puritan theologian Jonathan Edwards.

Life and Ministry of Edwards

Edwards was a product of the Puritan movement. His father Timothy (1668–1759) pastored a Congregationalist church in East Windsor, Connecticut; and his mother Esther was the daughter of the influential minister, Solomon Stoddard (1643–1729), known as the 'Pope of the Connecticut River Valley'. In his childhood home, he was steeped in Christian theology and trained in Latin, providing a robust foundation for his eventual studies at Yale College. After brief tenures as a pastor in New York and on the faculty at Yale, Edwards accepted a call in 1724 to join his grandfather at the Congregationalist church in Northampton. Within two years, Stoddard died, and Edwards was installed as the pastor of the largest church in the region outside of Boston.

His years at Northampton were remarkable in many ways. In the mid-1730s, a revival in his church drew international attention. The following decade, a visit from the British evangelist George Whitefield (1714–1770) sparked a second revival that spanned the colonies. While he continued to pastor his congregation, Edwards became an influential voice in the Transatlantic Evangelical world as he reported on the events and provided a theological framework for understanding this unprecedented work of God.

Interestingly, the revivals may well have laid the foundation for Edwards' eventual dismissal from Northampton. After his relationship with his congregation soured, he relocated his family to Stockbridge, Massachusetts, a frontier outpost where he served as pastor and missionary to the local Native Americans. In January 1758, he was appointed president of the College of New Jersey (now Princeton University), though his tenure would be brief. On March 22, Edwards died of complications surrounding a smallpox inoculation before most of his beloved family could even join him in Princeton. The correspondence surrounding his death illustrates the affection that existed between Edwards and his beloved wife, Sarah (1710–1758).

Recognizing his end was near, Edwards dictated parting words for Sarah to his daughter Lucy, declaring, 'Give my kindest love to my dear wife, and tell her, that the uncommon union, which has so long subsisted between us, has been of such a nature, as I trust is spiritual, and therefore will continue forever.'[1] Sarah's response to the news of her husband's death was preserved in a letter to her daughter Esther, which included the line, 'Oh, what a legacy my husband, and your father, has left us!'[2] It was a remarkable legacy indeed. Subsequent generations have profited from his careful theology and fervent attention to piety. Yet, no theologian is perfect and only Jesus maintained a spotless record. Just as pastors can learn from Edwards' many accomplishments, so too might they benefit from a careful study of his failures.

Dismissal from Northampton

It is difficult to imagine a pastorate that saw a combination of greater heights and more frustrating depths than that of Edwards' stint in Northampton. At the apex of his ministry there, the town was considered a model of the civic fruits that follow spiritual renewal. Yet his tenure ended in a near-unanimous vote to relieve him of his duties. The story of how Edwards' relationship with his people unraveled is a warning to any who would be tempted to underestimate the difficulties of persevering in ministry.

Edwards' public troubles with his congregation began in 1744 during what George Marsden has termed 'the "Young

---

1   George M. Marsden, *Jonathan Edwards: A Life* (New Haven, CT: Yale University Press, 2003), 494.

2   Marsden, *ibid.*, 495.

Folks' Bible" fiasco'.[3] A group of young men in the church were caught circulating medical books containing detailed descriptions of female anatomy and menstrual functions. The books were far from pornographic, but their contents supplied coarse jokes among the young men and armed them with cruel taunts of their female counterparts. Edwards' response was swift but tactless. In calling for an investigative meeting to look into the situation, he summoned a group of church members to his home by reading aloud a list of names that included both the accused and those called in to testify against them. As a result, several young men who had not been a part of the illicit activity, including the sons of some prominent townsfolk, were publicly humiliated for no reason. As the details of Edwards' misstep percolated among the town and the ordeal stretched into the summer, more and more Northamptonites came to view their pastor's response as overzealous and aloof. For his part, Edwards was disturbed not only by the young men's immaturity but by their audacious disregard for others. One of the more defiant offenders, who jokingly referred to the book as 'the Young Folks' Bible,' mocked the investigation publicly. In Edwards' mind, such brazen disrespect justified his actions, but many in the town disagreed.

Although the leading offenders were eventually required to make a public confession, the incident exacerbated interpersonal tensions boiling beneath the surface in the community. Never known as especially personable, Edwards and his people had been unable to agree on an equitable salary for years, an impasse compounded by rising inflation and the

---

3   Marsden, *ibid.*, 300.

growing needs of his expanding family.[4] Though a common problem in New England churches, this dispute was intensified by the Young Folks' Bible case and persisted for several years, setting the stage for Edwards' eventual dismissal.

Understanding the specific controversy that cost Edwards his job requires some context. Many congregations in eighteenth-century New England allowed individuals who regularly attended church and abstained from scandalous behavior to both receive communion and have their children baptized. The so-called 'Halfway Covenant' – originally proposed by Stoddard, Edwards' predecessor and grandfather – viewed the ordinances as a means of conversion, rather than as a privilege for the converted.

Edwards upheld this practice in his early ministry but grew increasingly unsettled about its legitimacy. In December 1748, he pivoted from established policy by suggesting that a recent applicant for membership must provide a credible confession of faith before being admitted to the Communion table. This view, while common among today's Evangelicals as well as many of Edwards' Puritan predecessors, was a major departure from Stoddard's policy. Furthermore, the policy change jeopardized access to the ordinances for many in Northampton.

While Edwards seems to have arrived at this position several years previously, he only made his views public after he and the congregation finally agreed on his salary. Now one of the most handsomely-paid ministers in the region, his lamentable timing compounded the sense of betrayal felt by his people. Not only was he was turning over long-standing practice and opposing his beloved grandfather, it appeared to his detractors

---

4   Marsden, for example, describes Edwards as 'brittle' and 'unsociable' (Marsden, *ibid.*, 344, 349).

that he had been less than transparent until his compensation was settled.

Once Edwards made his views known to his church, the town erupted. Although he quickly penned a lengthy defense of his position and later offered public lectures on the topic, few of his people engaged in meaningful debate as the controversy raged on throughout 1749. They felt burned by their pastor and viewed his shifting position as a final straw. The process dragged on for several months, but on June 22, 1750, some two hundred and thirty members of the church voted to remove Edwards from his post, with a mere twenty-three supporting the beleaguered minister.

While the people of Northampton were far from faultless in this episode, even those sympathetic to Edwards can recognize that he made several critical mistakes. His poor judgment in the Young Folks' Bible Case created an opportunity for resentment that seems to have never healed. His austere demeanor likely amplified the division, particularly as he disputed with the church about his compensation. His timing in announcing his new views on the Halfway Covenant was ill-advised and culminated a series of missteps that had unraveled his relationship with his people. As Mark Dever commented, 'Perhaps if Edwards had introduced this more gradually, matters would have turned out differently.'[5]

Edwards should be commended for his courage in attempting to change the church's membership policies. Thankfully his ministry there did not end in moral failure. In fact, as Marsden explains, 'Perhaps the greatest tragedy for

---

5   Mark Dever, 'How Jonathan Edwards Got Fired, and Why It's Important for Us Today', in *A God-Entranced Vision of All Things: The Legacy of Jonathan Edwards* (Wheaton, IL: Crossway, 2004), 135.

Edwards was that his pastorate was undone by his commitment to principle.'[6] However, much can be learned from how his Northampton tenure ended. Trust is a hard-earned but easily-wasted currency. Edwards failed to do the necessary relational work that might have prepared his people for his change of views. His dismissal is a reminder that foolish steps, even when taken in the right direction, will always have consequences.

Defense of Slavery

Getting fired from his pastorate was understandably a difficult trial for Edwards, but his greatest failure in ministry was unrelated to this incident. For those who look to Edwards as a model of faithfulness, the most difficult blight on his legacy is his relationship to slavery. Yale scholars Kenneth Minkema and Harry Stout provide a judicious verdict in noting that Edwards' views on the subject were 'fraught with tension and promise'.[7] Like most of his upper-class contemporaries, Edwards owned several slaves. In fact, it seems that he likely possessed at least one slave most of his adult life. Around 1741, he outlined a letter defending a fellow pastor whose congregation opposed their minister being a slaveholder. His primary argument was that those who condemned their pastor were hypocrites because they continued to benefit from the institution of slavery even if they owned no slaves themselves. Edwards' incomplete draft (no record has been discovered of the letter itself) is difficult to follow but it appears that he held to the popular view that domestic slavery was a necessary evil God could use for Christianizing the peoples of Africa, a common

6   Marsden, *Jonathan Edwards*, 370.

7   Kenneth P. Minkema and Harry S. Stout, 'The Edwardsean Tradition and the Antislavery Debate, 1740–1865,' *Journal of American History* 92, no. 1 (June 2005): 50.

argument most famously articulated in Cotton Mather's 1706 essay, *The Negro Christianized*.

Edwards was willing to challenge the prevailing opinions of his day. He rejected efforts to justify slavery by appealing to the practices of ancient Israel. He also vocally condemned the slave trade, calling it a violation of the biblical prohibition against 'man-stealing' (1 Tim. 1:10) and arguing that its continuation would undermine the global advance of the gospel. Minkema identifies Edwards' denunciation of the slave trade as somewhat unique in the American colonies prior to the Revolutionary War. His hope for the future millennial reign of Christ anticipated a day when the church would benefit from contributions by non-Anglo Christians throughout the world.[8] To this end, Edwards routinely exhorted the black members of his audience, admitted Africans into the fellowship of his Northampton congregation, and reported the sincere conversions of several blacks during the revivals.[9]

Still, Edwards' willingness to own slaves cannot be ignored. He may have spoken out against the slave trade but that did little good for Joseph, Lee, Venus, or young Titus, each of whom was a slave to the Edwards family at some point.[10] It is true that he seems to have treated them well and even labored toward their conversion, but such efforts do not validate their loss of freedom. The tensions in his views are clearer from a modern perspective than they seem to have been to him at the time. How could Edwards consider a black man a brother in Christ and yet function as if he were a lower class of human?

---

8   Kenneth P. Minkema, 'Jonathan Edwards on Slavery and the Slave Trade,' *William and Mary Quarterly* 54, no. 4 (October 1997): 828.

9   Minkema, 'Edwards on Slavery,' 829.

10 Minkema, *ibid.,* 825.

Why did his clear thinking on the slave trade not extend to the institution itself? These are questions Edwards never answered in print. It is possible that the incongruence never occurred to him. He lived in a day when most in his social stratosphere, and even many ministers, were slaveholders, convinced they were participating in one of the unfortunate realities of a fallen world.

This sobering acknowledgement presents committed followers of Christ with yet another question: How could a man so meticulously devoted to personal holiness fail to recognize his participation in such evil? Perhaps his failures serve us best when we allow them to supply a mirror for exploring our own. Might you and I possess similar blind spots in our own lives? Could our culture conceal the darkest depths of our own hearts? If Jonathan Edwards could ignore his own contradictions, surely we can as well.

Thorns and All

This chapter aimed to learn from the legacy of Edwards with special attention to his failures as a pastor. The goal is not to discredit the man nor to arrogantly look down on his weaknesses, but to examine them closely that pastors might be instructed today. This seems to be the path of wisdom commended in the pages of Scripture. In Proverbs 24, the wise sage describes his reflections upon passing by the field of a sluggard. It is unfruitful and unprotected. Thorns and thistles reign, bearing witness to years of neglect and poor decisions. But the wise man does not look past it. Instead, he considers how the vineyard got to this point and grows wiser through careful observation (Prov. 24:32-34). In this forgotten, fallow ground, he unearths the same gem he discovered in the industrious habits of the ant (cf. Prov. 6:10-11). Reading these two passages in tandem is encouraging to any who are face-to-face with failures, be it of their heroes or their own doing. Wisdom is found in both good and bad examples. In God's mercy, even thorns and thistles can serve as good teachers.

What can the thorns in Edwards' legacy teach us today? First, change takes time and *wise pastors lead slowly, with great care and attention to how their flocks are responding.* Even if Edwards was seeking to move his church toward a more biblical understanding of membership, he failed to help them see why. Once he fumbled the introduction, to their discredit, they were unwilling to hear the substance of his argument. Their response revealed some of the thorns that had grown in their relationship with their pastor. If Edwards could be distrusted by his congregation, so can anyone.

Second, *pastors must be vigilant to let Scripture rather than culture be the primary influence in their lives.* Edwards and many of his contemporaries failed to see the evils of slavery in part because they were blinded by the errors of their day. It is helpful to trace out how this happened, but it is paramount to consider how we can make the same mistakes. Historical context will never excuse heinous behavior. Are there ideas we hold dear today that might embarrass future generations of the church? Are we participating in activities or partnering with entities that reflect a greater adherence to our culture than our Savior? These are the questions every generation and every pastor must humbly answer.

Finally, it must be emphasized that *while Jonathan Edwards was far from perfect, God still saw fit to use him in a mighty way.* Ironically, his theological vision seems to have prepared the way for future generations to move beyond the atrocities he failed to recognize. Some of the New Divinity Men who followed in Edwards' footsteps became ardent abolitionists, including Samuel Hopkins (1721–1803), Lemuel Haynes (1753–1833), and his son Jonathan Edwards, Jr. (1745–1801), all of whom used Edwardsean principles to call for the end of slavery. As Sherard Burns has pointed out, 'The seeds of abolitionism flowed through the theology of Edwards.'[11] For that we can be grateful, even if those seeds failed to bear fruit in Edwards himself.

This chapter focused on the neglected fields of his personal life, but Edwards is of significance because his preaching, writing, and ministry produced such a bountiful harvest. A realistic portrait of his failures provides a more-balanced picture of his legacy. Moreover, it properly draws our attention away from Edwards to his God, a shift Edwards would welcome and celebrate. The glory of God – that great end of all God's works, according to Edwards – is so majestic that His splendor even shines through flawed figures. This ought to give hope to us all as we battle indwelling sin and difficult seasons in our own lives. If God can use a slave-owner to spark a revival, He might just use anyone.

---

11 Sherard Burns, 'Trusting the Theology of a Slave Owner,' in *A God-Entranced Vision*, 164.

14.

The Pastor and the Puritans: Concluding Reflections from Thomas Brooks

'A faithful minister must see before he say.' (Edward Marbury)

In *The Unsearchable Riches of Christ*, Thomas Brooks (1608–1680) outlines a series of observations from the text of Ephesians 3:8.[1] The value of faithfulness in the ministry of study and teaching in the life of the pastor is particularly noteworthy among Brooks' reflections, as it was also in our emphases here on Bible study (Goodwin and Charnock), teaching sound doctrine (Owen), and preaching (Perkins). Through the teaching and preaching lens, a faithful pastor is seen as one whose life aligns with his teaching, whose work is honorable, and whose gospel ministry will be rewarded by the Lord.

The 'Commanding' Lives of Faithful Pastors

In his explanation of how the pastor should 'preach Christ', Brooks stresses the need for both his *life* and *words* to be aligned in faithfulness and holiness:

---

1   'To me, though I am the very least of all the saints, this grace was given, to preach to the Gentiles the unsearchable riches of Christ' (Eph. 3:8).

The lives of ministers oftentimes convince more strongly than their words; their tongues may persuade – but their lives command.... What is that that renders the things of God so contemptuous and odious in the eyes of many people in this nation – but the ignorance, looseness, profaneness, and baseness of those who are the dispensers of them. Unholy ministers pull down instead of building up. Oh the souls who their lives destroy! These, by their loose lives, lead their flocks to hell, where they themselves must lie lowermost.... A painter being blamed by a cardinal for putting too much red upon the visages of Peter and Paul, tartly replied, that he painted them so, as blushing at the lives of those men who styled themselves their successors. Ah, how do the lewd and wicked lives of many who are called and accounted ministers, make others to blush!

Wicked ministers do more hurt by their lives than they do good by their doctrine. I have read of a woman who turned atheist because she lived under a great learned doctor who preached excellently – but lived very licentiously.... Every minister's life should be a commentary upon Christ's life; nothing wins and builds like this... 'Be an example to all believers in what you teach, in the way you live, in your love, your faith, and your purity.' (1 Tim. 4:12) 'Watch your life and doctrine closely' (1 Tim. 4:16).[2]

It is essential to heed Paul's admonition to Timothy, as we guard our living, believing, and teaching with great vigilance. The need to have all our vocational energies issue from life in Christ is why we focused here on proven voices who guide us to consider our piety (Bayly), prayers (Henry), affections (Sibbes), and family relationships (Gouge).

---

2   *Complete Works of Thomas Brooks* (Lafayette, IN: Sovereign Grace, 2001), 3:216-17.

The 'Honorable' Work of Faithful Pastors

This calling of a pastor is one of great distinction. The nature of pastoral calling (Bunyan), shepherding (Baxter), leading (Cotton and Winthrop), and evangelism (Eliot) are dimensions that point to the God-exalting soul work that we do as pastors. Brooks recognizes the gravity of our role:

> Their work is honorable. Their whole work is about souls, about winning souls to Christ, and about building souls up in Christ; and to these two heads the main work of the ministry may be reduced.
>
> 'Let him know,' that is, let him take notice that an honorable and glorious work is done by him. The soul is the immediate work of God; the soul is the image of God; the soul is capable of union and communion with God; the soul is worth more than a world, yes, than a thousand worlds. Christ prayed for souls, and wrought miracles for souls, and wept for souls, and left his Father's bosom for souls, and bled out his heart's blood for souls, and is gone to heaven to make provision for souls, yes, he is now a-making intercession for souls. All which speaks out the excellency of their office whose whole work is about souls.[3]

The 'Rewarding' Promise to Faithful Pastors

While Brooks speaks of the 'excellency of their office', we have all experienced indifference or antagonism on the part of others – a bitter word spoken, an untrue story recounted, a doubtful tone in response to a proposed direction for the future of the church. Sometimes these attitudes and actions are unwarranted, other times we have contributed by our own sin

---

3   *ibid.*, 224.

to unhealthy attitudes or even sinful actions, as we saw in our treatment of pastoral failure (Edwards).

Our true north is not the opinion of others or our ability to avoid missteps. The guide for our lives, through a diet of repentance and faith, is the Lord our God. He holds out the hope of unfailing reward in His presence:

Though the world crown them with thorns, as it did their Lord and master before them – yet God will crown them with honor: Dan. 12:3, 'They shall shine as the stars in the skies.' You know ambassadors have not honors while they are abroad – but when they come home into their own country, then their princes honor them, and put much honor upon them. So will God deal with his ambassadors: 2 Tim. 4:7, 8, 'I have fought a good fight, I have finished my course, I have kept the faith; henceforth there is laid up for me a crown of righteousness, which the Lord, the righteous Judge, shall give me at that day; and not to me only – but unto all them also that love his appearing.'

Ministers shall be rewarded according to their faithfulness and diligence, though some perish. It shall be with them as with vine-dressers. You know vine-dressers are rewarded according to their diligence and faithfulness, though some vines never bear, nor bring forth any fruit at all. As ministers are diligent and faithful, so the reward, the crown, shall be given forth at last. This is many a faithful minister's grief, that he takes a great deal of pains in rubbing and washing, as it were, to make souls white and clean, pure and holy, and yet they remain after all as black as hell; but surely their reward shall be never the less with God. The nurse looks not for her wages from the child – but from the parent. If ministers, like clouds, sweat themselves to death that souls may be brought to life, great will be their reward, though their souls should perish forever, for whom they have wept, sweat, and bled.... The world for all their pains will crown them with thorns – but God at last will crown them with glory; he will set a crown of pure gold upon their heads forever.[4]

Well Done, Good and Faithful Pastors

As pastors, we must be concerned with this one characteristic of our vocation – faithfulness. Sincere faithfulness is not easily wrought, as it can be attended to in certain spheres of life while neglected in others. To squarely fix our eyes and set our feet, Brooks' words may prove the most poignant of final exhortations:

> Ministers are ambassadors; and you know it is the great concern of ambassadors to be very faithful in their master's messages. God looks more, and is affected and pleased more, with a minister's faithfulness than with anything else. A great voice, an affected tone, studied notions, and silken expressions, may affect and please poor weak souls; but it is only the faithfulness of a minister in his ministerial work that pleases God, that wins upon God: Matt. 25:21-23, 'Well done, good and faithful servant; enter into the joy of the Lord:' a joy too big to enter into you, and therefore you must enter into it.[5]

May those breathtaking words from our God – 'Well done, good and faithful servant; enter into the joy of the Lord' – shape and sustain our pastoral work. Therein, indeed, is 'a joy too big to enter into you ... you must enter into it.'

---

4   *ibid.*, 225-26.

5   *ibid.*, 212.

Christian Focus Publications

Our mission statement —

STAYING FAITHFUL

In dependence upon God we seek to impact the world through literature faithful to His infallible Word, the Bible. Our aim is to ensure that the Lord Jesus Christ is presented as the only hope to obtain forgiveness of sin, live a useful life and look forward to heaven with Him.

Our books are published in four imprints:

CHRISTIAN
FOCUS

Popular works including bi-ographies, commentaries, basic doctrine and Christian living.

CHRISTIAN
HERITAGE

Books representing some of the best material from the rich herit-age of the church.

MENTOR

Books written at a level suitable for Bible College and seminary students, pastors, and other seri-ous readers. The imprint includes commentaries, doctrinal studies, examination of current issues and church history.

CF4•K

Children's books for quality Bible teaching and for all age groups: Sun-day school curriculum, puzzle and activity books; personal and family devotional titles, biographies and inspirational stories — because you are never too young to know Jesus!

Christian Focus Publications Ltd,
Geanies House, Fearn, Ross-shire,
IV20 1TW, Scotland, United Kingdom.
www.christianfocus.com
blog.christianfocus.com